ENDC

MW00479495

I've known Jason turner for many years, When I first met him, he was a young preacher with a heart to know God. When my husband would come and preach in the city that he lived in Jason would be in every service listening to every word, you could see a hunger to know God was gleaming in his face. When he decided to go to Oral Roberts University, I thought that it was the perfect choice for a young man with a heart for God to make.

Jason has always expressed a very sober and mature understanding of God's word. His insight into scriptures are very enlightening and his ability to do deliver God's word has always been powerful. I believe that God has anointed him for this generation to bring this clear and insightful revelation to the body of Christ.

I am so proud of him and the accomplishment of writing this book. I think it's very appropriate for what God has put in his heart, to be written in a book and be available for years to come. I want to congratulate him on such an accomplishment, and I encourage you to read this book. I'm sure that you will experience the same anointing and power of God through his writings that I have experienced for many years through the messages he has preached to the church I pastor. Your life will never be the same so I courage you to get this book!

PAMELA M. HINES
Author, *A Wife's Prayer* and *The Fabric of a Woman*
Owner | Perfect Peace Spa Collection
Pastor | Christian Faith Fellowship Church | Milwaukee, WI

Dream Again is the type of book that compels you to move from the place of complacency to the place of dream realization. Dreams that were lying dormant will receive fresh breath as the reader dives deeper and deeper into each chapter. Jason Turner masterfully takes the reader through the different stages of the dream process offering comfort and understanding to the discouraged dreamer, as well as tools and empowerment to the working dreamer. With a balance of both the practice and the supernatural, the dream inside each reader is bound to come alive. There is a dream inside of each one of us and *Dream Again* is a powerful tool to help each reader see his or her dreams actualize.

BRANDIE MANIGAULT
Author, *New Day, Fresh Start*
Teaching Pastor | ECOS Church | Irvine, CA

Dreaming is a beautifully intimate place between our God and us. In Jason Turner's book, *Dream Again*, you will hear one dreamer calling out to YOU to dream again while simultaneously being able to give you clear practical steps on the journey of dreaming. I recommend you read this book with expectancy and be willing to be challenged, encouraged, and awakened to all Christ has planted in you.

AARON DAILEY
Author, *Create in Me*
Lead Pastor | Redemption Church Alhambra | Phoenix, AZ

Reading this book empowered me to check doubt and fear at the door of my own heart! Dreams never expire but our doubt and fear definitely give them an expiration date! This book challenges us to not only resurrect the dreams we have but to remember that must have corresponding action in order to manifest the dream.

DELONDA OWENS TUCKER
Author, *The Wise Wife* | Phoenix, AZ

We all seem to start life with lots of hopes and aspirations. With lots of dreams. But over time, reality hits, and we struggle to live out many of those dreams. Here's an author with the biblical insight and practical advice to help us not only dream again, but truly live out those dreams by God's grace. I'm thankful to be on this journey with Pastor Jason and would encourage you to come along with me.

VERMON PIERRE
Lead Pastor | Roosevelt Community Church | Phoenix, AZ
President, Roosevelt Row CDC | Board Member, Surge Network

What starts as a spark will soon become a roaring fire! Pastor Jason Turner takes us on a journey from doubt to discovery, apathy to action and deferred, God given dreams to realized, God given purpose. His insights are timely and cross generations of believers everywhere who have muted the voice or ignored the push of the Holy Spirit to live out that huge idea only God can give. Prepare to not only dream it but LIVE IT! Thank you, Pastor Jason, for helping us walk out the big dreams only a big God can give.

STEVE PERKINS
General Manager | Automotive Franchise | Wauwatosa, WI

"Doubt is one of the devil's most used tool against the dream, and it must be violently and defiantly defeated with deliberate focus." This one line speaks to the entire intent of Jason to help the reader destroy complacency and annihilate the assumption that dreaming is for special people. *Dream Again* is a must read for a hope starved time in history. This book is one that I deem necessary.

DONELL COLBERT
Senior Pastor | The Chapel at Antioch | Antioch, TNMissionary

Dreams are often confused with visions. Dreams are the things that I've believe God gives you to exercise fearlessness and faith in the earth. I am a dreamer and being a dreamer has challenged me in every area of my life. I often say that dreams happen while you are sleep and visions happen while you are awake. This book by my good friend will cause you to awake and to put your dream into reality. It is filled with tools and biblical insight that will enrich and empower your journey to not fulfill the dream, but to dream again, again and again.

DARRYL E TUCKER
Music Producer | Musical Director | Phoenix, AZ

This book is motivating, inspirational and is filled with many points that has awaken the suppressed dreams that God had given me and I failed to act upon. Thanks for writing this and reminding us that it is not too late to re-ignite the dreams that have lain dormant in many of our lives. This book, along with the ministry that God has given you, has essentially provoked me to dream again. And I'm sure everyone who reads this will find themselves doing the same.

BOBBY DAVIS
Senior Pastor | Refreshing Springs COGIC | Riverside, CA
Regional Superintendent

This book speaks to anyone that has been challenged by having a dream yet being unable to fulfill it. *Dream Again* is informative and inspiring and will encourage you to move forward with the dream God has placed within you. Jason shares from his experience as a leader, husband, father, son and Pastor and accompanies this with his knowledge of the bible to share practical steps to harness the dream and fulfill it. This book is a must have for anyone that is ready to move on the dream inside.

DAVID ANDERSON
Senior Pastor | World Outreach | Maricopa, AZ

Dream Again reveals a practical proven path for personal empowerment and fulfillment to reach your God-given destiny. Pastor Jason Turner is a prolific preacher and teacher with great insight, vision and wisdom. This book will not only motivate one to 'Dream Again' but will inspire the reader to get up and run toward purpose despite any and all opposition. I highly recommend this valuable work to anyone that has an unfulfilled dream. "Dreams don't work unless you do." - John C. Maxwell

CATHY BANKS
Chief Financial Officer | Milwaukee, WI

There's a humanist approach to everything. Your God-given dreams aren't immune to this approach's Pastor Jason Turner exposes the opposition to attaining such marvelous, given dreams. He brings conscious awareness of these dream-killers. Now get them before they steal GOD's dream given to you. This is an encouraging read!

W. DOUGLAS TURNER
Senior Pastor | Christian Faith Fellowship Community Church | Chicago, IL

Never have we been in a place as a society where so many are searching for their purpose in God and not finding it because they dismissed or forgot the dream that God gave them. This book is a reminder to reconnect to that dream, the encouragement to move on that dream and a biblical based guide to accomplishment. So don't just read the book but absorb it into your heart and spirit and watch God bring your dream to reality as you follow the steps He has given Pastor Jason. I have no doubt that if you do, your testimony will be soon to follow!

TERENCE PRINGLE
Senior Advisor | Christian Faith Fellowship | Chandler, AZ
Business Owner

I encourage you, the reader, regardless of how you came about *Dream Again,* to take advantage of this gift you've been given. I pray that the soil of your heart is tilled to not only receive the information you're about to read; that you follow the instructions and take action!

As believers, the time for "a good read" is over. We need something that is going to challenge us as it heals us. You are embarking upon that journey, and it's ok, because God's timing is perfect, and your time is now.

Pastor Jason, I speak on behalf of the dad who is going to finish his business plan and submit it for funding, the mother of two who is going to finish her degree, the college student who is going to pursue her dream in spite of being told "that's not a career," all after reading this book...*Thank you.* Thank you for being transparent and vulnerable; for sharing what you learned so others can take action and see their dreams live. This was all a part of God's dream for you, for all of us who will read this book, and we're eternally grateful.

ANISSA PERKINS
Lead Intercessor | Christian Faith Fellowship | Milwaukee, WI
Project Manager | WI

I've known Jason Turner for many years, since the age of 19 he has consistently demonstrated a determination to preach the gospel and advance the Kingdom of God. One thing is for sure...Jason is a dreamer. When I say he's a dreamer, I'm not referring to someone who spends a great deal of time thinking about or planning for things he would like to happen but knows are improbable or impractical. No, Jason is a God dreamer. One who comprehends that God puts inside each individual His purpose for his or her life, and through faith is given the power to see that purpose come to fulfillment.

God is a dreamer, and few realize that His plans and purposes within you are essentially His dreams for you; what he envisioned and predestined your life to be before you were ever born. And make no mistake about it; God will place a demand on what he has invested in you because what is in you is designed to impact the world around you.

In his new book *Dream Again*, Jason Turner gives insight into the heart and mind of God while also looking at the heart of the dreamer. He walks with readers, helping those who may have lost sight of their dreams. Jason challenges us to focus on our dream instead of our many to-do-lists. He additionally supports individuals who may have abandoned their dreams, urging them to pick them up again, understanding that every single one of us has a right to see our dreams come true.

MELVA L. HENDERSON
Co-Founder | World Outreach Center | Milwaukee, WI
Author, *Fresh Baked Manna*

Jason Turner doesn't just write as a dreamer, but as a pastor and practitioner who has spent his ministry discerning God's voice to follow dreams through to reality. Dream Again is his encouragement to listen and respond to God's call in your life.

DENNAE PIERRE
Executive Director | Surge Network | Phoenix, AZ

I find that constant grumbling and drudgery makes life seem meaningless. It doesn't take someone who lives like this long to wilt intellectually and to develop a negative, cynical attitude towards life. Consequently, I whole-heartedly, recommend this book *Dream Again* to stop the grumbling and to begin the process of dreaming again!

ROBERT L WHITLEY
Pastor & Thought Leader | Chicago, IL

HEART ENDORSEMENT

God has giving us all a Dream, but it's our job to fulfill the dream that he has placed in us. I've been married to Jason Turner for 24 years and when God gave him the dream to write this book he and I had many thought provoking conversation about the dream. As he shared snippets of the book, tears began streaming down my face because I envisioned where I lost my dream. I watched him as he wrote the book through frustration, to waiting, to working, to complaining, to editing, to re-writing and to fruition. I'm glad he didn't allow the dream to die even when it looked unattainable, he kept working until his dream became a reality. Him dreaming and working his dream has reignited the dream within me.

RHODA L. TURNER
Conference Host | *Reflections Women's Conference*
Weekly Vlog and Monthly Columnist | *Rhoda's Reflections*
Pastor | Christian Faith Fellowship Church | Chandler, AZ
Wife of Jason N. Turner

Dream Again

© 2020, Jason N. Turner

Scripture quotations are taken from:

Amplified Bible (AMP)
Copyright © 2015 by The Lockman Foundation, La Habra, CA 90631. All rights reserved.

New International Version (NIV)
Holy Bible, New International Version®, NIV® Copyright ©1973, 1978, 1984, 2011 by Biblica, Inc.® Used by permission. All rights reserved worldwide.

The Message (MSG)
Copyright © 1993, 2002, 2018 by Eugene H. Peterson

New King James Version (NKJV)
Scripture taken from the New King James Version®. Copyright © 1982 by Thomas Nelson. Used by permission. All rights reserved.

The Passion Translation (TPT)
The Passion Translation®. Copyright © 2017 by BroadStreet Publishing® Group, LLC. Used by permission. All rights reserved. thePassionTranslation.com

For more information regarding the author, visit www.jasonturner365.org

ISBN: 978-1-09833-606-6
ISBN eBook: 978-1-09833-607-3

dream again

JASON N. TURNER

CONTENTS

FOREWORDS

I've been raised in church my entire life. When I was born, my parents were both born again believers and members of a Pentecostal church. So, from my childhood I was told the importance of the message of faith from my parents and that message shaped my relationship with Jesus Christ. Consequently, I gave my life to Christ at a very early age and even though I was walking by faith I wasn't entirely sure what that meant.

I believe that there are many born-again believers who know the importance of faith, yet they don't have the understanding of faith and how it works to our benefit. I believe that Jason Turner has been given revelation and insight to help born-again believers understand how faith works and how it best benefits us. It is God's desire for us to use faith to build his kingdom and to receive his promises.

I know that there are several books that speak of faith but there are very few that give experiential insight on having the faith necessary to fulfill your God-given dreams. If you believe God is a God of promise and that He watches over His word to perform it, then I encourage you to read this book. Be prepared to experience the blessing of knowledge, the ability to use your faith to trust God's word, and the instructions on how to apply faith properly to experience the full promise of God in your life.

I once heard an old preacher say that good preachers are a dime a dozen, but men of God are far and few in between. I believe Jason Turner is a man of God and this book is a word from God. Get this book in your library!

DARRELL L. HINES SR.
COGIC General Board Bishop
Author, *Resolving Conflict in Marriage*
Pastor | Christian Faith Fellowship Church | Milwaukee, WI

There are moments when it dawns on you that God has punctuated your timeline with a divine gift that made a difference in your journey. For me, one of those moments began over a BBQ lunch with a Pastor I was meeting for the first time by the name of Jason Turner. Within minutes, I had a sense I was getting to know someone with a unique grace and gift to unlock the doors of potential for people. Over the past few years, that impression has been proven true. Jason is a catalyst.

Pastoring in the same region with Jason has afforded me the opportunity to see the alignment of his walk and talk. That's important because un-walked talk is often flimsy ideas dressed up in appealing wrappers, empty of power to bring real or significant change and growth. *This is not one of those books.* The insights Jason shares in this book are inspiring, but they are also underwritten by a life that illustrates substantial results.

As you work your way through this book, you'll be both inspired by its content and equipped with practical steps to implement the process Jason outlines in its pages. My sincere hope for you is that you'd be willing to both "read" and then "do" what you discover along the way. If you do, you'll realize – like I did – that God has punctuated your timeline with a gift that will be a difference-maker in the story that is your life.

God often starts new seasons of growth and development in our lives by dropping the seed of His purpose and plan into our awareness. I believe this book is exactly that for you, no matter what season of life you are in. God's timing is always perfect. I encourage you to create some space in your life to let the insights in this book be the beginning of a new, exciting season of divine purpose. God created you to matter and the dreams He puts in your heart are tied directly to the path that He will lead you on to experience your greatest fulfillment in life.

Are you ready? It's time to "Dream Again."

DAVID E. WRIGHT II
Lead Pastor | Life Link Church | Gilbert, AZ

DEDICATION

To my mother, who survived, gave me to God and gave up a lot to ensure that I would have more than she had and to my grandmother who was an example of strength and kept me covered in prayer...they will both be dearly missed, and I look forward to seeing them again.

To my sister who has always had my back and I will always have hers; to Dorsey Christian III and Robert Whitley who befriended me at formative stages in my life and to Darryl Tucker who showed me 'how' to be a friend; to Bishop Solomon Smith who was my first example of a father and pastor and took me in as his own; to my in-laws who accepted me and took off the "law" and just brought me "in"; to Dad Hines who showed me what it really meant to be a man and validated me in that manhood when I needed it the most by calling me 'son'; to Mother Hines who showed me a love affair with the Father and who was the example of a true worshipper; to Emile & Cathy Banks who pushed and kept on pushing until I began pursuing greatness; to Bishop Darrell L. Hines who has mentored me from near and far and has, by his example, challenged me in ministry and demanded greatness from my life; to Pastor Pamela Hines who shows me the excellence of serving the Father.

Last but definitely not least, to my children, Gabrielle, Kennedy, Alivia and Abigail; thank you for making me laugh, teaching me compassion, and for letting me be to you what I never had, a father; and to my wife, Rhoda, who is my best friend, the sunshine in my day, and the love of my life, may I never know a day in life without your love being in it.

No man survives nor arrives on his own. He is a product of the people who have invested in his life. I could not possibly name all the people who have impacted my life but I am here today because of the investment of others. I would be foolish to think that I could have done it on my own. Thank you.

ACKNOWLEDGEMENTS

To Angel Freedom - Thank you for transcribing my heart from preached message to printed paper. Thank you for the reassurance that this platform of sharing God's word with His people is His heart for me. I look forward to doing this again and seeing all the books that will come from this venture!

To Brandie Manigault - I have learned through this process that the art of teaching/preaching is different than that of writing. I fully appreciate and respect your gift of communicating through the written word. It is because of your patience and willingness to pursue excellence that one of the dreams of my life has been fulfilled today. Thank you for seeing what I saw and most importantly for seeing what I could not see.

And to Angela (Gertz) Pfotenhauer – Thank you for helping me with my very first book that is soon to be published. It is because of our initial process from over 15 years ago that showed me this avenue was providential. I am thankful to God for our history. Your impact on our family during the Oshkosh season of our life has left an indelible mark that will never be forgotten.

INTRODUCTION

"The graveyard is the richest place on the surface of the earth because there you will see books that were not published, ideas that were not harnessed, songs that were not sung, and drama pieces that were never acted."
MYLES MUNROE

We are God's creations; each one of us crafted for a specific purpose. We begin our journey as dreamers in a world filled with possibility. Nothing seems impossible. The sky's the limit, and the stars are our playgrounds. Along the way we begin to settle into our day-to-day rhythms, and dreams are replaced with to-do lists. Routine takes over, and we find ourselves listening to the thoughts of limitations. Our purpose and desire lost in the blaring static of our lives. Yet still in our deepest places, we feel a push towards something more; a sense that we remain for something greater. We yearn most for significance instead of survival. It is time that we discover what was lost and diminished so that we may joyfully live out our purpose. It's time to dream again.

In the book of Genesis there is an amazing story about a young boy named Joseph. This story follows him from the age of 17 until the time of his death at the age of 110. And one of the greatest components of his story is the dream that God gave him. As we follow Joseph throughout the chapters, we see how God provides for him, as Joseph remains faithful to God and focused on the dream. There is always a process to anything worth having, and Joseph's story is a historical timeline full of principles, and if we learn them, they will help us navigate through our own God-given dreams. And prayerfully by following these principles we will begin to lay down historical markers that others can follow and see that their dreams are worth pursuing.

The desired intention of this book is to move you beyond inspiration and into a plan of action. People often say, "Where do I begin?" and I must admit that I asked the same question. You see, this book is the result of a dream! So I am not telling you something that I haven't lived, and I am currently living in the pursuit of the next dream. I am sharing with you what I have discovered and walked out every day. I have discovered that the place to begin is right where you are! Stop making excuses about what you can't do because of what you don't have. You are focused on the wrong thing. Instead focus on what you do have. Make up your mind that you will accomplish a little bit of your dream everyday. And let today be the day you begin. Decide to remove from the graveyard the contribution of your dream. It's the dream God gave you, and it's time to live it and not just wish it. Antoine de Saint-Exupery said that, "A goal without a plan is just a wish." The dream is your goal, and this book is a push towards the development of your plan.

May this book reinvigorate you and kick-start the dream in your heart again. There is more to life than just waking up, watching TV, and going to work. There is something that God has given you to do that no one else can do. But you must decide to dream again!

1

DREAM A DREAM

"Nothing happens unless first a dream."
Carl Sandburg

Dream: a series of thoughts, images, and sensations occurring in a person's mind during sleep; a cherished aspiration, ambition or ideal.

"And Joseph dreamed a dream… And he dreamed yet another dream…"
Genesis 37:5a, 9a

Everyone dreams, but not everyone dreams a dream. Closed eyes at the end of the night when exhaustion finally takes over leads your mind to wander and string together a storyline of pictures and words until a movie-like scene is created. Some dreams make little sense when we recall them in the morning, and we blame it on the nachos or pizza or excess lasagna we had the night before. Some dreams are so detailed and elaborate that they mimic our real-life situations. The thing you watched or read before falling off to sleep can impact dreaming. Dreams can also become nightmares, causing our heart rates to increase and a sense of panic to overwhelm us that jolts us awake. Everyone dreams, even though the details may be fuzzy or nonexistent when fully conscious.

Everyone dreams, but not everyone dreams a dream.

When a dreamer dreams a dream, something different is taking place. This dream is outside of the realm of environmental factors or familiar things that invade our subconscious. When a dreamer dreams, the Lord is imparting His dream for your life into you. When a dreamer dreams, God Almighty (the Ultimate Dreamer, the Creator) is revealing to you a picture of what He desires for you to be, to do, and to accomplish. You are being given access to His thought concerning you and His will for you. When God allows you to dream His dream, He is giving you a preview of a coming attraction. He is letting you have insight on what it is that He sees. When you dream a dream, you are receiving an all-access pass to the heart of the Father.

Let that settle in.

God Dreams

"All our dreams can come true. If we have the courage to pursue them."
WALT DISNEY

Dreams will always come before their reality. God-given dreams are designed to be a blueprint or a map to help navigate the dreamer to the point of realization.

Have you ever had a glimpse of inspiration for the future, a glimmer of hope of things to come? These thoughts have you so excited that you can hardly contain yourself. Like children in class whose teacher is fighting for their attention; you daydream about the business you want to start, the book you want to write, the person you want to marry, or nations you want to visit. You become obsessive over what you have envisioned but haven't seen yet. Your heart pounds at the thought of landing on foreign soil and eating authentic cuisines. Excitement overtakes you anytime someone mentions anything relating to a dance studio. You can picture the glass mirrors on the walls. You can feel the music blasting and hear the students' feet as they hit the ground with every beat and fluid movement. You have a "dream" jar on your nightstand that all your spare change goes into and as you watch it fill up you think about all that you're going to purchase for your new office space or the various types of coffee blends and espresso machines for your new coffee shop. It's going to be everything you've ever wanted and more. You are beaming with anticipation and filled to the brim with hope for your dream and your new future.

Then life happens.

Unexpectedly, your company includes your department in a budget cut, ultimately leading to your layoff. Your intended spouse doesn't want to get married anymore or a family member gets sick. None of these things were part of your calculations. They weren't accounted for when you were planning your future, but now they are here, and days that were full of light and hope, now seem dark and far away.

In the natural setting, when you dream dreams at night, the scene is set to darkness. The lights are off and your eyes are closed… darkness. It is most often the same with God dreams. God dreams are birthed and revisited in the dark moments of our lives. It is in the moments when things are at their worst, and we are ready to give up that the Lord brings those dreams that once lit up our hearts back to our mind. It's those dreams that will serve as a reminder of the greatness that resides beyond our circumstance, beyond the borders of other people's words, opinions, and speculations. It gives us a reason to get up in the morning when we would rather stay in bed with the curtains drawn. A God dream forces us to live and not just exist. A God dream will push us to a place where we are not just walking around numb, but living in purpose on purpose, because we're pursuing something. Dreams, the pictures in our minds that we are unable to shake, are the fuel that pushes us to get up every morning. They are the reason that we keep going when it gets dark all around us.

Your Dream is Yours

"I am successful because I never once believed my dreams were some-one else's to manage. That's the incredible part about your dreams; nobody gets to tell you how big they can be."

RACHEL HOLLIS

God's dream for you is His heart. It is His mind concerning us. The dream is God's way of sharing with us what He wants us to be and what He has for us. Your dream is His dream for you. Let this simple truth motivate you and push you to keep moving forward when life becomes difficult and it appears that you are not receiving the cooperation or support you so rightly deserve and need.

How many times have we had a brilliant idea and sat on it waiting for someone to open the door for us? I imagine it's more than we can count. It's uncomfortable to do something that we don't know how to do. God dreams will always be bigger than our ability to carry them out with our current capacity, resources, and abilities, but will never be bigger than His power and ability to make it happen. He will not show us something that He doesn't intend on doing for us. He will not tease us with the promise of Jeremiah 29:11 (NIV): *"For I know the plans I have for you,"* declares the Lord, *"plans to prosper you and not to harm you, plans to give you hope and a future."* Not one single Word He speaks will He dangle over your head like a carrot. NO! He is a good God who has good things for us and has every intention of giving them to us. And this includes the materialization of every dream that He has shown us.

But there is a part we must play in order to see the appearance of the dream. The dream will require work! God makes it clear in Habakkuk 2:2 (MSG) that the vision or dream is ours. It is our responsibility to (1) Get the vision, (2) Write the vision, and then (3) Give the vision.

And then God answered: "Write this. Write what you see. Write it out in big block letters so that it can be read on the run. This vision-message is a witness pointing to what's coming. It aches for the coming—it can hardly wait! And it doesn't lie. If it seems slow in coming, wait. It's on its way. It will come right on time.

Look at it this way: whatever it is that He has designated for you to do, is for you to steward and see it through. If you die leaving this earth without pursuing your passion with everything that you have, then you have robbed the world of being impacted by your dream. What dream are you taking to the grave because you were more concerned about what someone else would say or think? What God has placed in you is for humanity, and it's bigger than just one person. Your dream is designed to have a ripple effect. It is meant to be a blessing to your family, to your community, and to your city for generations to come. You are the one that God is calling to make a difference. Your yes to God unlocks opportunities for others.

Your yes to God unlocks opportunities for others.

You have to first grab hold of YOUR vision and fulfill it because no one else can do it for you. Your parents are not obligated to make YOUR dream and YOUR heart's passion come to life. Only you can do it. Your spouse is not responsible for YOUR dream. It's the dream that God gave you. It's part of the reason why He gave you life.

Dream Killers

"Share your dream with people who want you to succeed."
Bishop T.D. Jakes

Have you ever been so excited about something that you couldn't wait to share it? You received a promotion at work and rushed to get home to tell everybody. Or you got a call back for the play you auditioned for. Or you received your college acceptance letter in the mail. You can't wait to share the good news with somebody…with anybody. You finally have the opportunity to "spill the beans," and you share it with all the excitement you have bundled up inside you. Holding your breath, you anxiously wait for a response that matches the energy that you gave the news with only to be let down by their unenthusiastic "that's nice." Wow...a letdown of epic proportions! This is the feeling we get when we share our dreams with those who cannot handle what was given to us. Unfortunately not everyone knows how to appropriately celebrate the accomplishment of others. Their lack of excitement and word choice can leave us second-guessing the value of what we've shared. Is the promotion really a good thing? Am I really good enough for the play? Am I smart enough to make it at college? Can I really do what I envisioned? Am I worthy? Is my dream even good enough?

The book of Genesis gives us a great guideline and model to follow in the life of Joseph when it comes to dream killers. It shows us what to do in the event that doubt tries to set in. Let me tell you a secret...doubt will come. We just have to know how to navigate it, stay on track, and stay in the right frame of mind during these moments.

Joseph had a dream, and just like us, his dream excited him. So what did he do? He did what we all would have done, and probably have done on multiple occasions. He shared it. But he didn't share it with just anyone. No. Joseph shared it with those closest to him. He shared it with his brothers. Put yourself in Joseph's shoes. Who better to support me? *Who better to cheer me on? Who better to encourage me than my own flesh and blood, my brothers?*

Joseph made himself as vulnerable as he could and shared the thing that he held dear in his heart, the thing that's close to him, the thing that God spoke to him about at night—his dream. You have to be careful with your dreams and with whom you share them. Joseph released it into the hands and hearts of people he trusted; to people he thought would help him. Genesis 37:5 tells us that Joseph told his brothers the dream, but one verse before reveals to us how the brothers really felt about him.

> *"When his brothers saw that their father loved him more than any of them, they hated him and could not speak a kind word to him."*
> **Genesis 37:4 (NIV)**

Does that sound like someone that you should be sharing your heart and dreams with? Do any of these brothers sound like someone you should be vulnerable with and open up to regarding something that is dear to you? They couldn't even speak "a kind word to him." They didn't know how to celebrate Joseph and be happy for their BROTHER.

Was it that Joseph was so eager to share what the Lord showed him that he told the first people he saw? Or was it that he wanted his brothers' approval so bad that he went out on a limb, crossed his fingers, and hoped this would somehow make them proud of him? Or was he so caught up in what he had going on that he blinded himself to their actual heart concerning him?

Before you share your dream with anyone, it will be important to not only vet the intended recipients, but your motives for sharing as well. Why do you want to share this specific dream with this particular person? There will be times when, like Joseph, the people closest to you will be the ones that you gravitate towards first. Your heart yearns to tell someone about this amazing dream, and you think about your family, your friend that's been with you since kindergarten, or your mentor. But you cannot share your dreams with people just because of your proximity to them or because you have history with them.

You have to share your dream with someone who is unapologetically for you. Your dream supporters should cheer you on, champion you, praise you, challenge you, and most importantly, believe in you. And unfortunately, this is not a reaction that everyone knows how to have.

Be careful not to share your dream with dream killers. You cannot share your dreams with people who do not understand a dreamer because they themselves do not dream. Life can so alter people that they no longer believe in their dreams and consequently will not have the capacity to believe in yours. They can only operate from what they are familiar with. They won't get with you, won't support you, won't like you, and possibly, will try to sabotage your dream. They will unnecessarily say things like, "who do you think you are," or "what makes you think you can do anything different than us." But when you decide to start dreaming, you are making decisions that declare that you cannot remain where you are. There is somewhere else you are supposed to be and something more God has for you because He keeps showing it to you.

> **Life can so alter people that they no longer believe in their dreams and consequently will not have the capacity to believe in yours.**

I would encourage you to pray for those who, for reasons that are unknown to you, are unable to dream. Pray that God will fill them with hope. Pray that your journey will be an encouragement to them that they can do it and that they must begin to dream again.

(e)Motion Aside

"Parting is such sweet sorrow."
WILLIAM SHAKESPEARE

In order to get to the place where you're supposed to be, you have to, in one form or another, leave where you are. This may look like changing your surroundings and finding a workspace that is conducive to being creative. It may look like changing the people that you associate with, by spending more time with other dreamers.

Or leaving the routine of old spending habits in order to save towards the dream that your heart can't un-see. And on occasion it may mean that you put some space between you and your "brothers" (your family). In another story in the Bible, the Lord spoke to Abram and said,

> *"Go from your country, your people and*
> *your father's household to the land I will show you."*
> **Genesis 12:1 (NIV)**

He provided these instructions, and then in the next two verses He gave him the promise…the dream.

> *"I will make you into a great nation, and I will bless you;*
> *I will make your name great, and you will be a blessing.*
> *I will bless those who bless you, and whoever curses you I will curse;*
> *and all peoples on earth will be blessed through you."*
> **Genesis 12:2-3 (NIV)**

Danny Silk says in his book *Culture of Honor* concerning the Lord's command to Abram: "You and I gain identity from those we grow up with, it's very difficult for that identity to shift and expand once it's been established in the perceptions of those around you… You carry a particular identity in an environment filled with people who are very familiar to you." In other words, your people don't know how to let you go and grow beyond what they have always seen you as, and consequently there are times that God may require for you to leave so that you no longer see yourself through the limited scope of others, but that you begin to see yourself through the eye of God's dream for you. Unfortunately, there will be people who will only identify you with who you were: the irresponsible teenager, the professional college student, or so and so's child. Look how Jesus was responded to when He was around people that were familiar with Him:

When He had come to His own country, He taught them in their synagogue, so that they were astonished and said, "Where did this Man get this wisdom and these mighty works? Is this not the carpenter's son? Is not His mother called Mary? And His brothers James, Joses, Simon, and Judas? And His sisters, are they not all with us? Where then did this Man get all these things?" So they were offended at Him. But Jesus said to them, "A prophet is not without honor except in his own country and in his own house."
Matthew 13:54-57

Be comforted in knowing that those types of responses are not isolated instances with you but a condition of familiarity that is common with all people and cultures.

In order to make your dreams a reality, you may have to get away from some people. They are not equipped to go with you. They will always bring up the time you crashed your car when you share your dream of opening up a dealership. They will remind you of all the days you skipped school when you share your vision for after-school programs. This type of dream killer will try to get you to put your dreams on pause by casting seeds of doubt and unnecessary concerns in your mind about your past. The safest way to share your plans with dream killers is not to. Let the forthcoming materialization of your dream speak for itself.

Surround yourself with people that know how to dream. Surround yourself with people that believe in the God that's in you. Surround yourself with people that know how to talk in faith and believe for big things because they are an encouragement to you and help to keep you speaking life to your dream.

This journey and the pursuit of God's dream for you are not for the timid. You will be misunderstood and talked about. You will lose family and friends along the way. You will continually question if you have made the right move or if you made a mistake. But the thing that will comfort you through all the anxiety and angst is that you did not give yourself the dream. And that's why you cannot shake it. When you close your eyes at night and lay on your tear-stained pillow, the dream keeps popping up. In your darkest moments, it is God's word from His dream for you that will comfort you and embrace you when you are laughed at and scorned. Don't mistakenly think that this will be easy. If you think it will be easy, then I invite you to close this book and move on to something else because THIS dream will cost you every comfort. You have to be willing to be uncomfortable to chase after what God wants for you.

Dream Aloud

"Every great dream begins with a dreamer. Always remember, you have within you the strength, the patience, and the passion to reach for the stars to change the world."

Harriet Tubman

The thing about Joseph's dream was that Joseph's dream included his brothers, but his brothers didn't like their role in his dream. Not everyone will like or accept their role in your dream. People who are not used to dreaming can find it difficult to see a big picture and can very quickly get fixated on a small detail. You will not be able to convince people to have a vision for others when they cannot get beyond the sight of themselves. And because Joseph's brothers couldn't get beyond themselves, they were no help to Joseph, and actually became major obstacles, even though his dream included their deliverance. Try to remember that every Jesus has a Judas, every champion has a challenger, every climber has an obstacle, and every dreamer has a detractor; and your journey will be no different.

Every Jesus has a Judas...

You may be wondering how do you respond to these types of people. You respond to them by affirming yourself. Repeat after me: "I will keep going." You keep going. Don't stop and don't quit. The Father has given you a dream. He has given you an assignment.

He has given you a piece of His heart to make a reality in the earth, and when He gives you His heart it comes with everything that you need to accomplish it. He provides the vision, the finances, the resources, and the favor that will open doors. Discouragement will come. Obstacles will get in your way. Repeat after me: "I will keep going." People will question your abilities and your methods. Repeat after me: "I will keep going!" Let all of these things fuel you to dream harder, dream with more clarity, dream bigger, and dream with more detail.

Why is all this "repeat after me" stuff important? Because there will be times on this journey that the only word of encouragement you hear is what you tell yourself! You have to know how to get in a mirror, look at yourself, and speak your dream out loud so that you can hear it and see it being spoken. You have to learn now how to encourage yourself by speaking the dream to yourself. Unfortunately, there are times when we are hesitant to speak because we don't believe it. And if you don't believe it first, then there will be no need for anyone else to believe it second. This is why from the day we are born our mothers teach us our name by speaking it to us and continue to rehearse it in our hearing and sight until we learn to say it. Once we learn to say our name, we no longer have to be convinced of what our name is. And because we know what it is, we can be called by it.

Somewhere along the path of our lives we were spoken to negatively and we picked up a sequence of thoughts and beliefs that were grounded in someone else's impotence instead of constructed by God's potential. This is why you must speak out loud to yourself and remind yourself of the dream. Speak the dream to yourself so much that people who overhear you get sick and tired of your repetitive garb. Speak the dream so until people, due to childish immaturity, begin to tease you by no longer calling you your name but now they call you dreamer. The funny thing is that they think they are being hurtful, but the truth is that they, in their own irreverent way, are confirming what God has already said, what you agreed with, and what now the world is confirming.

As you dream and begin to take steps towards it, always make sure you continually check in with the Lord for confirmation and approval of what you are doing. He may show you that you are to start a business and work for yourself, but that doesn't mean He wants you to quit your job today. Make sure that you are staying in step with Him and His blueprints. Remain faithful to where He has called you and what He has placed in your hands to do while you pursue the dream. Do what He tells you until He tells you something different. Always pray…then obey.

Also remember that God will not show you what is next until you agree with what's first. He wants your response to be "I may not know how this is going to pan out, but God, I'm with you. Let's go. Let's do it, whatever it is you want to do." When you agree with God, when you partner with God, when you connect with God, when you cooperate with God, His response is, "Great, let me start showing you more." Often, as you dream one dream it will cause you to dream more. Something in you awakens (courage, determination, single focus, etc.) and makes the impossible seem possible.

> **Also remember that God will not show you what is next until you agree with what's first.**

Subsequently there will be times when the resistance against what God has shown you is so great that you are tempted to abandon the dream. But this just won't do! God will not change His mind concerning you because others don't have enough foresight to see you as something else, somewhere else. Come to God with the pain of the rejection and misunderstanding and see what He has to say. Just like in Joseph's case, God's dream for you is unrelenting, and instead of removing the dream he will cause you in the dark moments to dream another dream. Genesis 37:9 says that Joseph "had another dream." God will reinforce His plan for your life by causing you to Dream Again.

Chapter 1 Reflections

"All of our dreams can come true. If we have the courage to pursue them."
WALT DISNEY

Meditate on these scripture verses:

Genesis 37:4-9, Habakkuk 2:2, Jeremiah 29:11, Genesis 12:1-3, Matthew 13:54-57

Reflect:

- Everyone dreams, but not everyone dreams a dream.

- Your yes to God unlocks opportunities for others.

- Life can so alter people that they no longer believe in their dreams and consequently will not have the capacity to believe in yours.

- Remember that God will not show you what's next until you agree with what's first.

Questions:

What is the dream that is in your heart? What is the thing you see yourself doing if money and life responsibilities were not a factor? Who or what has been the main catalyst of doubt in your life?

_____

_____

_____

_____

_____

_____

_____

Prayer:

"Father help me to know that you have a plan for my life that is a result of your dreams for me. Help me to believe that I am worth that dream and that you did not make a mistake in entrusting this dream to me. Father I admit that life has tried its best to break my desire to dream and at times I have given in to the discouragement. But I commit to you today that as you reignite within me your dreams for me, I will trust you to give me the strength and courage to see them through to the end. Thank you for grace and mercy that are new every day. In Jesus name. Amen."

Activity:

Journaling is very important and therapeutic. Writing something down makes your thoughts concrete and actionable. There is something permanent and real to an idea that has been written down. That writing becomes a reminder to what is possible. That written testament becomes encouragement to you on what your goals are and where you are going when things appear to be their darkest. Take the next few moments to write down your dream and date it. This may feel uncomfortable but take time to search through the surface answer and dig into the details of the dream. Where are you? What does it look like? What does it smell like? What's the temperature where you are? Who is with you? And who did you have to leave behind?

_____

_____

_____

_____

_____

_____

_____

_____

_____

2

EVERY DREAM HAS STAGES

"A dream doesn't become reality through magic; it takes sweat, determination and hard work."
COLIN POWELL

Your dream, a preview of the future, is to encourage you that where you are is not the end. There is more for you. There is more for you to do. There is more for you to obtain. There is more for you to accomplish. Where you are currently financially, relationally, and spiritually is just the foundation for where you are going. Do not give up just because what you may be experiencing does not line up with what you have burning in your heart. Do not throw in the towel. Do not quit, and do not be quiet. Do not relinquish your passion for helping widows and orphans to someone who doesn't have a heart for the disenfranchised. Do not hand over your burden for global relevancy to someone who can only think locally.

The truth is that it will get hard. It will get hard to hold onto hope at times when sight and vision do not align. But you have this hope that you can grab onto with both hands and cling to when doubt, worry, concern, or the many questions arise:

"Being confident of this very thing, that He Which hath begun a good work in you will perform it until the day of Jesus Christ:"
Philippians 1:6

Being confident: Being self-assured
He: God
Who has begun: Started
A good work: The dream
In you: YOU
Will perform it: Will finish what He started

In other words: Be self-assured that God, the One who started this whole process by giving you the dream in the first place, will most definitely finish what He started. That should bring you some peace when you hit those creative roadblocks or come face to face with writer's block. You **Here's the secret to success: Stay with God.** will undoubtedly face challenges as you produce but remember everyone faces challenges. The real challenge lies in what you do with and in the challenges. Here's the secret to success: Stay with God. He gave you the dream, and He will give you Heaven's intelligence on how to complete it. He has skin in the game. His Word is on the line. He cannot lie, and the improbability of your dream will not be the thing to make a liar out of Him. Neither your inabilities, fears, inadequacies, nor your challenges are powerful enough to take on and defeat His perfect record of success.

> *"God is not a man, that He should lie; neither the son of man, that He should repent: hath He said, and shall He not do it? Or hath He spoken, and shall He not make it good?"*
> **Numbers 23:19**

Did you know that YOU are on God's mind? He intentionally created you to carry out a specific mission on earth. He has a dream about you. He thinks about you, and He doesn't just think average thoughts about you. No! He thinks good thoughts. Prosperous thoughts. Hope-filled thoughts. He thinks about your now, but He also thinks about your future.

*"For I know the thoughts that I think toward you, says the Lord,
thoughts of peace and not of evil, to give you a future and a hope."*
Jeremiah 29:11

The beauty of Him focusing on your future is that He stands
outside of time and can orchestrate divine appointments for you to
walk into. He arranges for you to sit next to a fellow dreamer at your
local coffee spot, and immediately you begin swapping stories about
your next big projects. And as you share your heart, the fire inside
regarding the dream starts to burn hotter and the urgency to take the
next step consumes you.

Many people contemplate the meaning of life; wondering,
"WHY am I here? WHY was I born?" Can I tell you that the answer
to that question lies in the realization and actualization of the dream
placed inside of you as a seed. Who you are and what your purpose
in life is cannot be defined by anything or any one other than the
Lord. You are living because you were on God's mind before you
were born.

*"Before I formed you in the womb I knew you; Before you were born I
set you apart; I appointed you as a prophet to the nations."*
Jeremiah 1:5

In the above scripture reference, the Lord took the time to
assure Jeremiah of WHO he was, WHO created him, and WHY. I
can imagine the conversation the Lord has with Jeremiah and Him
saying, "I SEE YOU. I KNOW YOU. I CREATED YOU. I CALLED
YOU. That thing that's burning inside of you, that dream, that pull
to do something that seems bigger than you…I did that and no one
else." Just like He confirmed and affirmed Jeremiah in his call, He
will do the same for you as well. Keep your ears open not just to His
roar but also to His gentle whisper. There will be multiple opportunities for you to wrestle with your call, to go back and forth with
the Lord concerning your dream in the pursuit of the goal. This

wrestling tension is what makes you and develops you in the process from conception to actualization.

Have you ever heard the expression, "I could do it with my eyes closed" or "It felt like I was on autopilot"? It is said because someone has done something so many times that it's almost a no-brainer for them to execute it again. They have practiced a song on the piano so many times that their fingers automatically hit the right notes at the right time producing a beautiful tune. Basketball players practice their free throws for so long standing in the same spot, holding the ball the same way, and releasing it at the same arc each time that it comes with ease the more they do it. They have put in the work, wrestled with technique, and made mistakes, but after all of that is done the result is a nearly perfect performance.

The process of wrestling may not feel good, but it is necessary for growth. There needs to be a wrestling to make it feel worth it in the end. When things are too easy, we tend to think that we did it in our own strength. But when we have to wrestle with something, even if it's a mental wrestling, and we finally hit that place of accomplishment, we then realize that the Lord breathed on us and empowered us to do it. It's that realization that becomes muscle memory for the next time we face a roadblock. It's a faith builder. We wrestle. We contend. We fight. We do everything that we know to do in our own strength, and then we surrender it, allowing the Lord to bring a harvest from our labor and investment. This process, when executed well, produces in us the faith to not give up the next time. Instinctively we know that if the Lord came through for us the last time we dreamed a dream, then He will do it again. Our faith is continuously being built up like muscle memory every time we face a challenge. "Practice makes perfect."

Time Waits for No One

"Time is what we want most, but what we use worst."
WILLIAM PENN

There are certain dreams that He has for you to accomplish, but one paramount fact that you need to know about these types of dreams is that they are time sensitive. Due to the urgency for what you must accomplish, you cannot drag your feet and take forever to begin the process. There are cures for cancer and other diseases that are locked away in dreamers! And the people whose lives that are affected by such illnesses are not afforded the same luxury of time while you decide if you want to participate in your own dream. The reality of someone's destiny being tied to your obedience has to compel you to take action now! Step out in faith and be proactive in seeing the vision through. If God has given you a dream, it is because He sees the bigger picture of the impact it will have. You have to get to work! You have to get back to the laboratory! You have to start grinding and hustling and GET IT DONE!

> **The reality of someone's destiny being tied to your obedience has to compel you to take action now!**

"There is a time for everything, and a season for every activity under the heavens:"
ECCLESIASTES 3:1

It is one thing to have a dream and keep it on repeat in your head, replaying it over and over, while you picture what it will be like when it comes to pass. It's another thing to actually live out in real time, the thing that's been playing like a movie in your head. It's time to live the dream; to take it from seed to harvest. It is time to go from thinking, "what *could* happen" to "what *is* happening."

STAGE ONE: The Pit

"Stars can't shine without darkness."
UNKNOWN

At the onset of Joseph's dream, he well-meaningly shared it with his brothers. Unfortunately, his brothers in turn hated him even more than they already did because of it. Their family dynamics were what we would describe as dysfunctional at best. It was full of jealousy, envy, strife, favoritism, daddy issues, and more. The brothers' dislike for Joseph was so intense that they devised a plan to not only get rid of him but to kill his dream. Their goal was to thwart any hope of Joseph becoming anyone or doing anything in life that would bring him any more recognition than he had already received.

"Then they took him and cast him into a pit.
And the pit was empty, there was no water in it."
Genesis 37:24

In the first stage of dreaming you are going to have to deal with the pit. The pit will teach you perseverance. Joseph's brothers cast him into a pit that was empty and had no water. The pit was dark, isolated and contained no visible resources. It was the last place he wanted to be in. There may be times when your dream leaves you in what seems like a dark, isolated place with limited resources. The people that you assumed would celebrate you or help you will disappear. Our critics will lean towards the tendency of letting their personal life experiences shape their opinions

The pit will teach you perseverance. of what we are doing. They may even go so far as to try and discredit you in an attempt to keep others from casting their support

towards you. Some may plot and scheme to get footing in their case against you. Your pit will seem lonely, but be assured that even though you are alone, you are not without an advocate in the shadows.

"When Reuben heard it (the plan to kill Joseph), he delivered him out of their hands, and said, "Let us not kill him." And Reuben said to them, "Shed no blood, but cast him into this pit which is in the wilderness, and do not lay a hand on him" - that he might deliver him out of their hands, and bring him back to his father."

Genesis 37:21-22

Joseph had someone on the inside looking out for him. He had someone on his side, making sure that neither he nor his dreams were destroyed because of someone else's insecurities. Not everyone that seems like they are against you, are really against you. Some may have to leave the room to get a head-start in order to be able to help you further down the road. They may not know how to stand up against the crowd, but they have every intention to not let the crowd succeed in their plans to destroy you.

Your job, in the face of adversity, is to hold on to the dream and don't let it go no matter what people say or do. You have to decide that no matter what may arise you will stay the course in order to fulfill the dream that God has for you to fulfill. Pits will come and pits will go. The pit is not ideal, and it is not comfortable, but it will only be as miserable of an experience as you allow it to be. You and you alone control how you get through that experience and what you will learn from it because the pit doesn't last forever. Just like everything else you face in life, the pit is only a season. The question you must ask yourself is this, "When I come out of this pit, will it be with or without my dream?"

> **Joseph reconciled within himself that he would remain faithful even in the dark.**

Joseph reconciled within himself that he would remain faithful even in the dark. He would continue to believe even if he was the only one. He would do the work to stay alive even when the resources were scarce. He had faith to believe that the One who gave him the dream would be faithful to him. You are dreaming a dream that you didn't conceive on your own. It was given to you, and the One who gave it to you is responsible for unfolding the vision, resources, and necessary favor. Your obstacles are conquerable when you stay focused. Keep your eyes on the Light in your dark moments. You are able and capable because of God to get through this season as long as you persevere in the hard times and don't give up.

You Will Be Mishandled

"Your greatest test will be how you handle people who mishandled you."
UNKNOWN

It is almost inevitable that at some point you will be pushed down, pulled up, and then passed on.

"Then many night traders passed by, so the brothers pulled Joseph up and lifted him out of the pit and sold him to the Ishmaelite's for twenty shekels of silver. They took Joseph to Egypt."
Genesis 37:28

It is a part of the process that is unavoidable. A mistake that people in a pit make is in thinking that everyone who helps them out of it is on their side. If you are not careful, you will trust that their help is genuine. You will believe that they didn't mean to sabotage your business proposal. They didn't mean to discredit you when they were telling your future business partners about your inexperience. They didn't mean to pull back their support when you reached out for help. Obviously, it was all a misunderstanding because here they are now with their hand out ready to pull you out of the pit that they put you in. They will help you, but their focus is not on your break-through but in taking your pit experience to a darker level.

What they don't know, as they are executing their plan for your demise, is that the dream doesn't die due a dark place. Those things are only temporary setbacks that ultimately strengthen your ability to execute and sustain the dream. The time in the pit showed

Joseph that the Lord would deliver him out of dark situations and that although things seem insurmountable, that he shouldn't give up hope.

As long as you keep your dream submitted to God (the Dream Giver), nothing that happens to you regarding the dream will catch Him off guard. He will utilize every pit experience to grow our trust in Him, which will ultimately lead to the fulfillment of the dream. There is a lesson in every setback that you face. With each "no" from potential investors, you are building stamina and courage to keep going. When your resources seem scarce, remember that He is your provider. When writer's block hits and the words for the next book or song won't flow, learn how to lean into His voice. Every dream is His word in the form of a seed and His word will not return to Him *"empty, but will accomplish what [He desires] and achieve the purpose for which [He] sent it"* (Isaiah 55:11 NIV). God's Word is His promise to us. And God protects what is His.

Roll Up YOUR Sleeves

"Promises are invitations to potential. It's our 'yes' that make it possible."
BILL JOHNSON

The dream He gave you will not work itself. It will not happen just because He gave you the dream. It requires your "yes." It requires

The dream He gave you will not work itself.

your "yes" when things are going well and when you face challenges. It requires your "yes" when the ideas are flowing smoothly and when they seem to come sporadically. It requires your continual "yes" until you have successfully and effectively accomplished what He put in your heart to do. Your "yes" is the key to unlocking His protection plan against any attempts to permanently derail you. He protects what is His when you are doing what He asked of you to do.

It is the promise seen in the seed of your dream; the scene of pictures in your mind and the knowledge of its impact in your community that will keep you steady in the pit. Survival is in part based upon you knowing, deep down, that in the end it will all work out the way it is supposed to.

You can do it. You've got this. God's got this!

"Present with me in the pain and patient with me in the journey."
KAYLA STACK

Know that the pit is not your promise. The difficult spaces are not your end. It is a place to develop character in you. It is designed to teach you how to maneuver in the hard times. It is not your final destination. It is not your home. Genesis 37:28 says that the people who purchased Joseph took him to Egypt. Joseph may not have known it when he had the dream, but going through the pit provided the vehicle to get him to the next stage of the fulfillment of the dream. Sometimes the pit is allowed because it provides the transport to get you to a place that you would not have voluntarily gone to. Just as in the life of Jesus Christ and all believers, you must go down before you can go up. This principle is called the J Curve. In

Sometimes the pit is allowed because it provides the transport to get you to a place that you would not have voluntarily gone to.

order for there to be a resurrection, there must be a burial. In order for there to be a dream, there must be a dark moment. And in order for the dream to be realized, there must be a pit. It may seem like you are going down, but the current trajectory is necessary in order to gain the correct momentum to catapult you to the next place.

"...the J-Curve because, like the letter J, Jesus's life went down into death, then up into resurrection. Just like the earthly life of Jesus, the J

ends higher than it starts. It's the pattern not only of Jesus's life, but of our lives—of our everyday moments."
PAUL E. MILLER

More often than not, God will tell us where He wants us to be in life—the end goal—but we are not aware of the geographical location. We see the landscape of the scene but don't have the coordinates. So there has to be a well-orchestrated plan in place to get you from the pit to the promise. It may not be a comfortable journey. It may not be ideal. It may seem unconventional. It may feel like it is meant to break you, but submit to the journey and you will arrive at your destination.

Let me caution you. It will be easy to give in to the pit and stay there longer than need be. DO NOT stay in the pit. Shift when it is time. DO NOT get comfortable in what you may view as disappointments. It will be tempting to build a tent and settle in to the routine of being turned down, rejected, setbacks, slow roll-outs, etc., but DO NOT let the pit suck you into staying longer than the season necessitates. Own where you are for as long as you are there, and when it's time to move on, move on. Even though hardships existed, and he felt every one of them, Joseph did well in that he remained focused. He kept his eyes on the promise. The dream continued to burn in his heart. Keep your eyes on the dream. Along the journey, questions will arise. I'm sure that Joseph had a few questions. "Why Lord?" "Why me?" "When will my breakthrough come?" "When will people believe in me and support me?" Is it ok to ask the same questions? Yes! Give a voice to your concerns. Speak to the Lord about what's on your mind and in your heart. He is always speaking and is eager to speak to you about you, because…

"…every single moment [He] is thinking of [YOU]"!
Psalm 139:17 (TPT)

Chapter 2 Reflections

"Stars can't shine without darkness."
UNKNOWN

Meditate on these scripture verses:

Philippians 1:6, Numbers 23:19, Jeremiah 1:5, Genesis 37, Psalm 139:17

Reflect:

- Here's the secret to success: Stay with God.
- The reality of someone's destiny being tied to your obedience has to compel you to take action now!
- The pit will teach you perseverance.
- Sometimes the pit experience is allowed because it provides the transport to get you to a place that you would not have voluntarily gone to.

Questions:

Do you find yourself currently in the pit phase of your dream expedition? If so, are you willing to forgive those who, for whatever their reasons were, tossed you into a pit scenario? What are your pits, and can you see how God is utilizing them to work perseverance into your life?

_____

_____

_____

_____

_____

_____

Prayer:

"Father help me to forgive those who have had a hand in placing me into a pit scenario. Allow me to know that all things work together for good to those who love God, and are called according to purpose, and that this is one of those things. God, I trust you even though I may not understand or agree. I submit to your plan for my life. You are the potter and I am the clay. Use this season in my life to shape me and mold me into what you would have me to be. In Jesus name. Amen."

If it helps, write the name of the person or persons that you are asking God to help you forgive. You will know when forgiveness has fully taken root because this list will turn into a list of people that you are praying for God to bless.

_____

_____

_____

_____

_____

_____

Activity:

Forgiveness is essential for a dreamer who realizes they have a God-given dream. Lists of grudges to keep, axes to grind, and people to get even with is not the resolve of a person with a God-given dream. Today, let's begin the practice of letting things go, in hopes that it builds within us the discipline of forgiveness.

This may sound elementary but the impact on your life will be profound. On a piece of paper write down the names of those who you believe have wronged you. Then ball up that piece of paper and throw it in the garbage. This movement symbolizes your commitment to forgive and let it go. Now you may have to repeat this a few (hundred!) times but it will be the physical practice needed to help shape your mental disposition regarding that person or thing.

3

THE PROPOSITION

"Every morning you have two choices; continue to sleep with your dreams or wake up and chase them."

UNKNOWN

God-given dreams are given by God. It sounds simple, but this one truth needs to be a continual reminder and focus. The fact that your dream was given to you by God needs to remain your central focus. When you have a focus, something to hold on to, that one thing will keep you going on good days and on bad days. When you remember the source of what you have in your heart you will not rely on your own interpretation of the dream. You will seek the giver of the dream for His design and His steps of execution.

Dreams are a preview of a coming attraction. A dream is designed to light up your heart with so much hope and excitement that you cannot contain it. He shows you the end at the beginning. He shows you the people connected and impacted by you. He shows you the **Dreams are a preview of a coming attraction.** nations you will visit and the programs that you will start. God shows you all of this now so that you will not give up in the middle of the process.

In the last chapter we talked about the pit. We saw how the pit aids in the development of focus; a core competency that is needed to access the dream. It is part of the process that grows us and strengthens us. We also touched on the idea that the pit is NOT our place of promise. But there has to be something between what we are currently experiencing and the final destination. It is a temporary port that ultimately provides transport to new geographical spaces.

Let's recap Joseph's journey thus far…

- Joseph was home and happy. He was hated by his brothers but loved by his father.

- Joseph dreams a dream and tells his family. His brothers hate him more and plot against him.

- Joseph's brothers throw him into a pit. They decide to make money off of him and sold him to a group of Ishmaelites heading to Egypt instead of letting him rot and die in the pit.

STAGE TWO – The Proposition

"Never give up on what you really want to do. The person with big dreams is more powerful than one with all the facts."
ALBERT EINSTEIN

The second stage of the dream is what I call "the proposition." The Oxford Dictionary defines proposition as *a suggested scheme or plan of action…(v). especially in an unsubtle or offensive way.* The proposition is a result of where you are.

"Now Joseph had been taken down to Egypt; Potiphar, an officer of Pharaoh, captain of the guard, an Egyptian, bought him from the Israelites that had taken him down there. The Lord was with Joseph, and he was a successful man and he was in the house of his master the Egyptian."
Genesis 39:1-2

The proposition picks up when you have exited the pit and the joyful reality that the Lord is with you kicks in. Joseph, even though he was gaining popularity and favor while living in the master's house, was still a slave. He was not a free man able to come and go as he pleased. He wasn't able to do what he wanted when he wanted. He had to answer to multiple masters. He still had to endure slave conditions. In spite of his circumstance, the Lord was with Joseph.

You have exited your pit, but the pressures from "being sold into slavery" are everywhere. It may not make any sense. You may be pondering a series of questions and thoughts:

- Why does my family hate me? What did I do to them?
- If God is with me, then why am I still enslaved?
- When will this all end?
- I barely made it out of the last season, how am I supposed to get out of this season?
- Now what? What now?
- Why me?
- Why did the Lord allow all of this to transpire this way?

Joseph, even as a slave, even under the pressure of his new "job," even witnessing the injustices surrounding other slaves in comparison to his treatments, had God in his corner. The Lord makes the difference. You can endure anything that comes your way, even setbacks and things that don't make sense, when the Lord is with you.

Knowing that the Lord is with you is comforting, but at the same time it can leave you feeling emotionally distressed and full of questions. When you look at His omnipotence matched against your current situation, it seems unfair. We would like to believe that His greatness and power would outmaneuver what we are going through and bring immediate freedom! But often times we incorrectly equate God's presence with us as His deliverance for us.

Let's look at the definition of presence and deliverance. According to the Oxford Dictionary, presence is defined as the state or fact of existing, occurring, or being in a place or thing; whereas deliverance is defined as the action of being rescued or set free.

Your deliverance from a place or situation is dependent on His presence but is not guaranteed at a specific time or in a specific way. You cannot have deliverance without His presence, but you can have His presence without His deliverance. He will not deliver you from what you are currently facing until all that you need to get from the situation is developed in you. Early release from

You cannot have deliverance without His presence, but you can have His presence without His deliverance.

a season is forfeiting treasures that were meant to be attained and is a guaranteed "redo." You will inevitably face a different obstacle in order to get His desired outcome for your life.

His deliverance from a situation is two-fold. He will use your current reality to deliver OUT of you bad habits, idiosyncrasies, and proclivities that are contrary to His nature and His design for you.

"Then God said, 'Let Us (Father, Son, Holy Spirit) make man in Our image, according to Our likeness [not physical, but a spiritual personality and moral likeness]...'"
Genesis 1:27 (AMP)

God wants to first spiritually get things out of us while we are in so that He can inevitably physically deliver us from what we are in. Submitting to the process is essential to successfully completing the journey. You can complete the journey but not maximize every opportunity to learn and grow. A college student can pass their strategic management course with an A while taking every opportunity to dig into the material, ask questions, join a study group, and absorb all of the material. Or they can pass with a C by doing the bare minimum in order to get through the class without having to retake it. At the end of the day, whether the student graduates with an A or with a C, they both have spent the same amount of time and money on the class. This is how our seasons of life are. We can do the bare minimum in order to move on or we can maximize the season and gain all of the wisdom that the season has for us.

The Lord is omnipresent. He is always with us. He is present. With His presence comes all of whom He is. He doesn't come with healing, salvation, joy, love, and leave behind peace, strength, and hope in Heaven. When He comes, He brings all of who He is with Him. God is with us, and He is working on us. It may not be comfortable, but God knows exactly what He is doing. He is taking the chisel to your life and breaking off the things that will bring jeopardy to you later. Submit to His presence in this tough season and know that your deliverance has already been scheduled.

The presence of God does not always signify the deliverance that you picture in your mind. We want God (the Great Rescuer!) to come to our defense, fight our battles, end the hard season, shut the mouths of the accusers, vindicate us publicly, and promote us in front of all those who doubted us! But what the Lord wants to do in us is more important than what we want Him to get us out of. For every word that is spoken about you by your enemy, the Lord is developing in you a soft heart while giving you thick skin. For every offense felt on the present journey, the Lord is trying to deliver you from the un-forgiveness that has settled in your heart over the years. For every correction received, the Lord is delivering you from the need to be right all of the time.

Here are some clear indicators that the Lord wants to deliver you from something:

- Someone's presence alone rubs you the wrong way
- You have a hard time submitting to authority
- You get an immediate attitude when someone's name is mentioned
- Anger and rage rise up when you think about the past
- It is hard for you to trust people at their word
- You are constantly seeking someone's approval

I believe God will allow situations to happen because He wants to take you back to your "factory settings" that more accurately reflect His image and likeness and less of what past traumas have shaped you to become. Surrendering to the process of this type of deliverance is going for the A in the class. And after the work is done, you've gotten all you can get out of it, the end of the course will come and you will be graduated (naturally and spiritually)!

Enduring all that Joseph endured at the hands of his brothers, the Ishmaelites, and those assigned to watch over him in Potiphar's home, there was plenty of room for bitterness, anger, rage, and resentment to settle into his heart. He had many occasions in which to contemplate how to get revenge, if he ever was freed from his prison, but instead he chose to remain yielded to the plan of the Lord for his life and trust that his life was in the Lord's hand. Because of this, the Lord favored him where he was. It is important to note that the Lord didn't wait until He delivered Joseph from his enslavement to favor him. He blessed him in the midst of a season that was originally intended by people to keep him in bondage and oppress him.

"And his master saw that the Lord was with him and that the Lord made all he did to prosper in his hand. So Joseph found favor in his sight, and served him. Then he made him overseer of his house, and all that he had he put under his authority."
Genesis 39:3

Get Out!

"God doesn't want managed expectations. He's looking for crazy faith."
UNKNOWN

Have you heard of the expression "blessed to be a blessing"? The dream that God gave Joseph didn't start with him but actually began with his great-grandfather. God gave clear instructions to Abraham with a promise (a dream) attached that Joseph begins to live out years later.

"Get out of your country, from your family and from your father's house, to a land that I will show you. I will make you a great nation; I will bless you and make your name great; and you shall be a blessing. I will bless those who bless you, and I will curse him who curses you; and in you all the families of the earth shall be blessed."

Genesis 12:2

Have you ever considered that your dream is a continuation of a dream from a previous generation? Maybe you are the first to graduate college in your family and it was a dream come true. But your dream coming true was also a dream of your great grandparents, that because of their sacrifices, someday their grandson or granddaughter would graduate college. You saw the dream clearly, but your great grandparents dreamed it first. Just as with this example you have to know that you are a giant piece to the puzzle and your configuration within the landscape of time is essential to the whole puzzle being completed. You are part of the human race and you have a specific leg of the race to run. The baton is being passed to you, and the previous runners are expecting you to do your part just as they did.

"Wherefore seeing we also are compassed about with so great a cloud of witnesses, let us lay aside every weight, and the sin which doth so easily beset us, and let us run with patience the race that is set before us..."

Hebrews 12:1

There are various components to a relay race, but one of the most crucial ones is being able to get out of the starting block. Someone has to get out first. This requires a posture that is only necessary for this runner. If anyone else takes this posture, they will fall because it is not the natural posture of the rest of the runners. Remaining runners run upright and have their own special set of disciplines that must be met in order to have success. But getting out of the blocks requires going first, being on your hands and knees, and the ability to change position at a moment's notice. Why is this important? Because your God-given dream may require you to have to get out. As Abraham was instructed, you might have to get out and away from the things you are familiar and comfortable with in order for God to show you something entirely different. It is hard to see something new while looking at the same old view. Sometimes God requires a change of scenery in order to plant you in a new context that allows for a blossoming uninhibited by the shade of others. This is not to say that there is something wrong with where you are. The same shade that protected and comforted you in one season can unintentionally in the next season block the sun and become shade that hinders the potential of your growth.

Sometimes God requires a change of scenery in order to plant you in a new context that allows for a blossoming uninhibited by the shade of others.

Getting out of the blocks first, or trailblazing, is difficult. It takes what others would call, "Crazy Faith!" Not everyone can lead by leaving, and it may cost you everything. I am telling you what I know personally because my family and I lived it for years as I personally went through the stages of pursuing the God-given dream. You will be misunderstood and talked about. You will trade comfort for discomfort, fine dining for packaged noodles, frequent flyer miles for long-distance road trips, clothes shopping for window shopping, vacations for 'stay-cations' (at home), and date night will become good-night! We lost financial security, emotional stability, a house, faith in God, companionship of dear friends, company car, perks and benefits, medical insurance, etc., and no one, but my wife and I, will ever know the depths of the cost. Again, I lost a lot BUT I gained a focus and a trust in God that is proven. I gained a prayer life. I gained GOD!

I remember a story that my mentor, Bishop Darrell L. Hines, would often tell while preaching. There was a time when he was approached by a young man that asked if he could pray for him that he could have the same type of anointing he had. So Bishop Hines began to pray, "Father, I pray that this young man gets struck by lightning and lays dead for 45 minutes. I pray that when you give him his life back that you let him lose his memory. Then after you restore his memory let him lose his job. Let him then lose his insurance and have to go on public assistance just to be able to eat. Let him then almost lose his wife to asthma and let his child be born with an incurable disease…"

The young man screamed, "Stop. Wait a minute preacher! I asked you to pray that I have your anointing and ability to preach like you."

Bishop Hines responded, "Young man, I am. You can't have my NOW and not be willing to go through what I had to go through to get it!" After that the young man gathered his things and quickly walked away. You see, we all want the end that we see of someone else's story, which is living in the dream, but we have to be willing to submit to our journey and run our race in order to get the ending that is prepared for us. You cannot have my dream; you must go live out yours.

The Power of Being Faithful

"God is not a deceiver, that He should offer to support us, and then, when we lean upon Him, should slip away from us."
AUGUSTINE

God always has been and always will be faithful to us. It is this faithfulness to us that should provoke from us faithfulness in return to Him. We should note that being faithful to God has benefits. God shows favor to those who are faithful to Him, and we can see it in our lives via two main elements: faithfulness produces opportunity for position and that positioning comes with influence.

Everything from the moment that your season begins until the moment that your season concludes hinges on this one thing… FAITHFULNESS.

What does it look like to be faithful? It looks like being loyal, constant, steadfast, and committed. It looks like keeping your word even when it costs you more than you anticipated. It means showing up to work every day on time even when they continue to disrespect you. It means staying when you want to go, loving when you want to hate, forgiving when you want to hold a grudge, and following when you want to lead.

You just have to remain faithful to God and your current assignment. Again, according to the Oxford Dictionary, the word remain not only means to stay in a place, but it means that you *"continue to exist, especially after other similar or related people or things have ceased to exist."* All the variables in your environment may change, but you have to remain fixed. The presence of certain individuals at work may provoke anger amongst the employees, but you are tasked to be a peacekeeper. You are to remain hopeful when all seems hopeless, calm in the midst of chaos, loving when hate fills the room, and quiet in speech around gossipers. Faithfulness is not just seen in how you respond to the things that directly benefit you, but it is also seen in your faithfulness to something that is a benefit to others. Let's be honest…it's easier to be faithful to a project when you know that the results of the project will cause you to receive a raise. But can you be just as faithful when the intended result is to see your co-worker get a raise? And not just any co-worker but the one who has covertly tried to get you demoted? Can you be faithful then? God's measure of your faithfulness is in your response to what He has said to you and not to how you feel about what He said. Be faithful to God and the assignment He has placed in your hands; regardless to where it takes you or who it directly benefits or how long it takes.

Remain faithful to God, and He will open doors for you. You don't have to force them open. He will announce your presence and make it clear to everyone that He is with you. Your commitment is the key to God repositioning you for the next season. You don't have to do any of the work. Let God do it. Let God open the doors. Let

God open the eyes of the people around you. Let God change their hearts. Let God bring about the changes needed to shift your season. When He does it, it takes the pressure off of you to perform for anyone. No one will be able to say that you manipulated anything to get the desired results. Your hands will be clean of any accusations. For every raise and promotion, your response is, "to God be all the glory." When people praise your talents and abilities, your response is, "Thank you. It's all God." With favor comes attention. As people give you attention, you turn the attention back to God. As people recognize you, you recognize Him. As people honor you, you honor Him. When they point to you, you point to Him.

You have now gained access to influence. You have worked, hustled, grinded it out, remained faithful and steady, and it appears that you are doing well in your season. You are not yet to the desired goal and you haven't arrived at the picture in your dreams, but you have made significant progress from the day you had the dream until this moment. You are content but not complacent. You are maximizing your moment, while still keeping your eyes on the end goal. I love the following scripture because it shows how our faithfulness to God can be a blessing, not just to ourselves, but to others as well. Joseph's obedience and faithfulness to his season not only blessed him, but it caused Potiphar's house to be blessed as well.

"So it was, from the time that he made him [Joseph] overseer of his house and all that he had, that the Lord blessed the Egyptian's house for Joseph's sake; and the blessing of the Lord was on all that he had in the house and in the field."
Genesis 39:5

God is our source, and he will orchestrate things around us to be a resource to us. As long as you remain faithful to God, He will bless what you are faithful to. God choose to bless Potiphar's house because it was a resource to Joseph that provided employment, housing, food, and purposefulness. As people promote you, God will increase His blessing on them because of His purposes with you. How they treat you can be a determining factor in how God responds to them. Whether people realize it or not, your faithfulness to God was the blessing that kept their business opened and thriving. It was for your sake that God did it! Please realize who you are to God and how much He will shine on you and others because of your love for Him and faithfulness to Him.

Here Comes Trouble

"If destruction fails to entangle us, distraction will do its best."
BETH MOORE

Joseph was faithful to God by being faithful to what Potiphar placed in his hands. Because of this approach, he quickly became a rising star to Potiphar. Potiphar began to trust Joseph with more and more, and that trust eventually led to Potiphar placing Joseph over all his estate.

Once you gain momentum, those who do not wish you well will rise to the surface with vocal opposition and sabotaging actions. They will come with seemingly good intentions, but it will be steeped in their own self-preservation and advancement. The tactic of distraction is to cause you to respond to a stimulus in a manner that is outside of your character, compromising of your integrity, and intent on destroying everything you have worked hard to accomplish up to this point. Be assured that if the enemy shows up to proposition you, that the offer is steeped in an agenda that will produce a negative outcome for you.

The thief does not come except to steal, and to kill, and to destroy..."
John 10:10

Joseph was only propositioned because he was doing well in Potiphar's house.

"He left all that he had in Joseph's hand, and he did not know what he had except for the bread which he ate. Now Joseph was handsome in form and appearance. And it came to pass after these things that his master's wife cast longing eyes on Joseph and she said, "Lie with me.""
Genesis 39:6-7

Joseph was a slave with power. He was not a free man with power, yet Potiphar's wife still saw him through the lens of position and power and she gravitated towards him. Potiphar's wife was not a stranger. She was in his world. They, although limited, had interactions throughout the day. They passed each other in the hallways of her estate. Potiphar's wife saw how handsome Joseph was and was additionally attracted to the influence he was accruing. Favor and purpose is attractive to the onlooker. It will take you from being "average" to "exceptional" in the eyes of the one trying to proposition you. The proposition may not come as blatantly obvious as Potiphar's wife was with Joseph. Yours may come in the form of an old friend you haven't talked to in a while reaching out. It may be an old boss inquiring of your work status. Or an old love interest may resurface by sending you a probing text. People who once overlooked you will suddenly take notice when things begin to change favorably in your world. Heads will start turning in your direction when you go from being the one needing assistance to the one who is now providing assistance for others. The quantity of people who want to be around you will increase, but the quality of those people will be noticeably deficient. This type of uninvited attention should cause the warning lights on your internal dashboard to go off. When people only want to spend time with you when you are doing well, their intentions are misaligned with your core values and the dream you carry. As easy as it is for them to be attracted to you when you are doing well, it will be just as easy for them to want nothing to do with you when you are no longer doing well. Discernment will be key in this part of the journey because it will help you to know who to trust with your dream, its details, and the secrets of your "behind the scenes" journey.

If there is a question in your mind as to whether you are where you should be, then allow the surfacing of the proposition to be a clear indication that you are right on schedule. Remember, the presence of the proposition comes as a direct correlative response to your position. The person propositioning you will try to get you to go against what you know is God's path for you. This person will suggest that you stand when you know you should sit, or to be quiet when you know you should speak. These people will try to bait you into old habits, and it will come packaged as if they are looking out for your best interest. It is this type of subtle and persistent manipulation that the enemy will use to get you to lower your standards and abandon your dream.

There has to be a resolve within you to not lose sight of who you are and who you are becoming as a result of the dream. Joseph was able to resist Potiphar's wife because in his heart he knew who he was and who his God was. His God had a track record of delivering him out of seemingly hopeless situations. He had proven to Joseph multiple times that He could be trusted to have Joseph's best interest in mind. When his brothers devised a plan against him for their gain, it was God that delivered him out of the pit. When the slave traders brought him to Potiphar's house for their gain, it was God that elevated him. When it looked like all was lost, God was there. When Joseph could have given up and given in to depression, resentment, or fought those who used him for their personal victories, he reverently turned his face away from his circumstances and turned it towards His God. Joseph consequently could stand in confidence that Potiphar's wife's advances would not be the end of him, because he trusted in a God who had consistently had his back time and time again.

This type of resolve within you will give you the courage to look at your tempter and declare your conviction. The first encounter with the propositioner is the most important. It sets the stage for your boundaries. Joseph's response to Potiphar's wife was this:

"Look, my master does not know what is with me in the house, and he has committed all that he has to my hand. There is no one greater in this house than I, nor has he kept back anything from me but you, because you are his wife. How then can I do this great wickedness, and sin against God?"

Genesis 39:8-9

Joseph was clear on his faithfulness to Potiphar, but most importantly, to God. And he wasn't afraid to speak up for either of them. Be leery of the person who is asking you to join them in being unfaithful to the thing they are supposed to be faithful to. You have to be secure in who you are and why you are doing what you are doing. Joseph's response to Potiphar's wife spoke loudly of his character and integrity.

> **Be leery of the person who is asking you to join them in being unfaithful to the thing they are supposed to be faithful to.**

Joseph was fully aware that Potiphar was not keeping tabs on him throughout the day. He had Potiphar's trust. Potiphar gave him great latitude to do what needed to be done without having to check in or give an account for his actions. With that level of freedom, he also knew that he could get away with compromising if he wanted to. When you reach a level of freedom to the degree Joseph had, you become less regulated by outside sources. No one will notice if you come to work late. No one will pay any attention if you cut corners on your project. It will go without detection if you take more than your share out of the tip jar. Your commitment to your personal integrity is the only thing that will keep you doing right behind closed doors. The temptation to give in will be unrelenting at times. It will try to find your weakness and exploit it, but you have to remain steadfast in the face of the enemy's assault. Believe it or not, but Joseph's refusal of Potiphar's wife made her want him even more and she continued to speak *"... to Joseph day by day"* (Genesis 39:10). But Joseph refused to compromise and put the future of his dream in jeopardy by giving in to this moment.

Joseph had permission to access all things without restrictions except Potiphar's wife. Adam and Eve had permission to access all things in the garden except the tree of the knowledge of good and evil. There are consequences to accessing the forbidden thing. For Adam and Eve, their disobedience cost them a great deal, but it also had lasting implications for the entire earth, thus resulting in our need for a Savior for redemption. Unlike Adam and Eve, Joseph valued God's word to him over the temptation put in front of him. His disobedience would have changed the future of Israel. He would have derailed the plan of restoration for his brothers' deliverance. The twelve tribes of Israel would not have existed. The whole trajectory of Jesus Christ

> When God is positioning you to do something it is always bigger than just you.

would have changed because one person said yes to a sin. When God is positioning you to do something it is always bigger than just you. It is more than just where you are. There are people, communities, cities, and nations connected to your obedience. Your children and their future are engrafted in the choices you make every day.

The dream that you dream is affected by your obedience to God and the seasons He has you in. When your dream requires you to study, will you study or put it off? When your dream demands that you discontinue certain unfruitful relationships, will you stop calling and texting or will you holdfast to them because you don't see the harm? When your dream asks you to dream a little more, will you pull out a pen and paper and brainstorm ways to expand or will you give into discouragement because you haven't seen any tangible results thus far? There is a price to disobedience. But there is a reward for obedience and faithfulness.

I learned a very important lesson early on in the formation of my personal life and ministry pursuits. Everyone affectionately called my wife's uncle, Uncle Governor, and if you had the pleasure of knowing him his name was a perfect fit because it was both familiar and regal at the same time, just as he was. He lovingly and graciously treated everyone like family, and whenever he spoke, his commanding voice demanded your attention. He was the preacher's preacher and a wealth of biblical knowledge. But there was one lesson in particular that he shared with my mentor, Bishop Darrell L. Hines, that according to him, helped shaped and protect his ministry. Well, if it was good enough for my mentor, then I definitely wanted to know what it was. It was a simple lesson with three points. It's often that the most profound things are found in simplicity. The lesson was a mantra for life, and he would say, "There are three things in life you have to guard against: sex, pride, and money. These three things have brought down great men on the cusp of fulfilling their dreams. These three things are the devil's most used and successful tools and are undefeated if you give in to them." What Uncle Governor was telling us is that we must guard ourselves against the plan of the enemy to derail us with sex (the unlawfulness of), pride (the excess of), or money (the love of). Guard against these things and position people in your life who can be real and transparent with you as they aid in helping you to guard your life.

Joseph was able to guard against all three of these areas in his life because he kept his focus on honoring God and securing the dream. Secure the dream at all cost. It may cost you comfort now, but the dream being realized is absolutely priceless. Thank you, Uncle Governor, for the practical wisdom and thank you, Joseph, for the example that gives us historical context and biblical application.

Please remember, the proposition has everything to do with getting you derailed from destiny. And once you are derailed, the proposition and the propositioner will be gone. The devil's tactics have not changed and have been successful since the beginning of time. Don't be foolish enough to think you will be the one person in humanity that can indulge in the proposition and it not impact the position of your dream. See the temptation for what it is, stand your ground, confront it, and maintain your position of pleasing the Lord in pursuit of the dream He gave you.

Chapter 3 Reflections

"If destruction fails to entangle us, distraction will do its best."
Beth Moore

Meditate on these scripture verses:

Genesis 39, Genesis 12:2, Hebrews 12:1, John 10:10,

Reflect:

- Dreams are a preview of a coming attraction.

- You cannot have deliverance without His presence, but you can have His presence without His deliverance.

- Be leery of the person who is asking you to join them in being unfaithful to the thing they are supposed to be faithful to.

- When God is positioning you to do something it is always bigger than you.

Questions:

What has taken an interest to you in this season that ignored you in previous seasons? What is the endgame of those who are trying to entangle themselves to you? Is that person or thing worth forfeiting all of the advancements you have made to this point and possibly put the dream in jeopardy?

_____

_____

_____

_____

_____

_____

Prayer:

"Father help me to stay focused. Allow me to be wise in my dealings with people and help me to see their true motives and intents. Father, we have come to far for me to now let go of your hand and rest my head in the lap of destruction. Thank you for discernment and the grace needed to deal with temptations. Thank you that your word tells us that with temptations you will make a way of escape. Help me to see the door of escape and give me the dexterity to run towards it. In Jesus name. Amen."

Activity:

When we fail to count up the cost, we end up spending and sacrificing way more than we intended. Make a list of the pros and cons to help you determine if the distraction is worth the investment. There is always an exchange with a transaction; the real question is, what are you losing by making this transaction.

_____

_____

_____

_____

_____

_____

_____

_____

_____

_____

_____

_____

_____

_____

_____

_____

4

THE PRISON

"Still, I rise."
MAYA ANGELOU

Your dream should feel bigger than you. It should feel unimaginable, incomprehensible, and unattainable. When you think about what God has put in you to accomplish, the first thing that you should think is "HOW." Our minds are so limited by the boxes that we live in that it is hard to wrap our brains around the "bigness" of what God is showing you to do. "Maybe He got it wrong. Maybe the dream was meant for someone else. Clearly He knows what I'm working with and how impossible it is for me to accomplish what I see." This is a perfectly normal line of questioning. It's unfathomable to our finite minds that we could pull off such a massive feat. Fortunately, we don't have to understand any of it to do it nor do we have to do it alone.

"Trust God from the bottom of your heart; don't try to figure out everything on your own. Listen for God's voice in everything you do, everywhere you go; He's the One who will keep you on track."
Proverbs 3:5-6 (MSG)

All we have to do is trust in the ability of God, the Dream Giver, to show us what we need to do. It is easy to pinpoint a God dream because the dream is more about others than it is about yourself. The desire to bring fresh foods into urban areas or opening up a youth center in underprivileged neighborhoods is for the benefit of that community and is larger than your immediate family. Yes, you will benefit from what you are called to do. The Lord will not inspire you to do something great and leave you un-impacted. He has no desire for you to be average. He chose you. Let that sink in for a second. Of all the people on this earth, He called you to start the dance studio. He called you to build the orphanage. He called you to launch the pop-up shop. He called you to open the restaurants or plant a church. And because God is perfect in all things, He did not make a mistake and doesn't regret burning the dream into your heart.

> It is easy to pinpoint a God dream because the dream is more about others than it is about yourself.

Nothing catches the Lord off guard. He is fully aware of the challenges that may come your way. He is well acquainted with the moments of doubt and fear and questions of self-worth, but He never waivers from when He makes a decision. Your dream was God's decision and it is specific to you. Your neighbor's dream is specific to him. Your cousin's dream is specific to her. You can't do their dreams, and they can't do yours. Your dream is your dream. There's something that you've been designed for that no one else can do. This is the God-given dream!

Chapter 1 described your dream as a preview of what's to come. It is similar to when you go to the movies. You get into the theater, settle down in the chair with your popcorn, and then the lights start to dim. Then suddenly the screen comes on and images start to appear. The sound is all-encompassing as you feel the vibration go through your body. You are mesmerized by the flashing colors, the action scenes, the love scenes that wrap around you like a warm blanket, and the music that makes you sway without effort. Then at the end of the preview the words "COMING SOON" slam against the black screen and silence fills the theater as it sinks in, followed by quiet chatter amongst friends saying, "I'm going to see that when it comes out." What we don't realize in that moment is that the preview we just sat through is of a movie not yet finished. It is still in the making. It is not ready for the public to witness just yet. The preview is designed to create hype around its release.

Your dream is much like the movie preview. It is to build excitement in you for what's to come. God wants you to see what He sees in you and for you. He wants to show you the impact that you will have and the footprint that you will make in the earth. The only thing that is missing in the production of your dream is your participation. You have to actively engage the dream in order for the preview to become a reality that audiences can someday enjoy and be impacted by.

STAGE THREE: The Prison

"Although the world is full of suffering, it is also full of the overcoming of it."
HELEN KELLER

The lack of success on the part of the propositioner in their attempts to get you to compromise, will cause them to elevate their attack with false accusations in order to damage you in the eyes of other people.

"The Hebrew servant whom you brought to us came in to me to mock me, so it happened, as I lifted my voice and cried out, that he left his garment with me and fled outside"
Genesis 39:17

Unfortunately, this false accusation opens the prison doors for Joseph. When Potiphar's wife couldn't get her way with Joseph, she turned the system against Joseph. Always know that the true heart of the propositioner will be revealed when you reject their proposition. The full weight of the political and judicial systems has been leaned against Joseph and he now finds himself incarcerated! Joseph is in jail for doing the right thing and staying faithful!! That's how it may appear, but even in the worst, most unthinkable and unbearable moments, God is still sovereign and has a plan. This is the time to guard your heart so that you do not do or say anything against God that you will regret later. Remember that the devil cannot stop the dream, but he will try and break the heart that the dream has to come through. Guard your heart!!! Have you ever been in your car alone and stuck in traffic? All you see in front of you is a parade of red brake lights while your rearview mirror shows the faces of frustrated drivers behind you. There doesn't seem to be a path forward, and you cannot go backwards. This is what the prison stage is like. Your destination is ahead, but you cannot move. You are all alone, and you cannot go anywhere. You feel stuck!

> **Remember that the devil cannot stop the dream but he will try and break the heart that the dream has to come through.**

Health experts and environmentalists say that you should never drink water from a stagnant source. Any place where the water sits still with no outlet is a breeding ground for diseases. Drinking from stagnant waters will make you sick. The prison stage is dangerous because you will be tempted to partake of the stagnant waters of the season, and it will poison you. The stagnant waters surface in these various ways but don't drink of it: anxiety, loneliness, self-loathing, and doubt. Anxiety will try to dominate your calm nature and level-headedness. Loneliness will try to take over by implying that no one is ever on your side or believes in you. Self-loathing will surface, tempting you to believe you will never be more than a prisoner at the mercy of someone more powerful than you. Doubt tries to creep in by replaying negative conversations and jockeying for them to take the place of you meditating on your dream and on God's word. You will be tempted to give in and give up and relegate yourself to this moment in time. But remember, where you are is not who you are! Dreamers will always face obstacles, no matter how great they are, as steps that allow them to rise to meet their goals.

The pressure to quit has intensified because when you enter the prison you are getting closer and closer to the actualization of the dream. It may not LOOK like it, but you are closer than ever before. In prison, you will experience favor and setbacks, friends and pseudo friends, freedom and bondage. The way that you handle the prison stage is important because it is the bridge to your promised land.

Mishandling the uncomfortable and inconvenient moments of the prison will cause a forfeiture of certain elements upon your release. Ultimately what you forfeited will only be able to be gained by going through another prison cycle in a different season.

You should have an internal resolve as you are being escorted into the prison that "I have made it through the Pit. I stood my ground with the Propositioner. I am innocent of the accusations and implications! THIS PRISON WILL NOT SHAKE ME. No matter what comes, I will remain focused. I will keep my eyes fixed on my God and trust Him to deliver me in the right time. The dream is not dead as long as I refuse to not let it or me die in this stage."

4 Things to Note Concerning the Prison

"You receive the favor of God in your life when your heart, words, and actions line up with the Word of God."
BILL WINSTON

1. Faithfulness to God in this stage produces favor anywhere that He places you.

When Joseph was a promoted slave in Potiphar's house, he was given favor and access to all things in the house except Potiphar's wife. Potiphar's wife was the only thing that was withheld and forbidden for Joseph to touch. The accusations against him were a direct assault against this instruction. In that day that type of betrayal would have called for Joseph to lose his life, but instead of death, Potiphar put him in prison. Just as the Lord was with him in the pit, and just as the Lord was with him at Potiphar's house, Genesis 39:21-23 says,

"...the Lord was with Joseph and showed him mercy, and gave him favor in the sight of the keeper of the prison. And the keeper of the prison committed to Joseph's hand all the prisoners who were in the prison; whatever they did there, it was his doing. The keeper of the prison did not look into anything that was under Joseph's authority, because the Lord was with him; and whatever he did, the Lord made it prosper."

The Lord was with Joseph every step of the way. He gave him position, power, and authority in every environment. He promoted him and made people responsive to him EVEN WITH his enslaved title. Joseph was surrounded by other prisoners that had offended Potiphar, the law, or even the King but not unto the penalty of death. He wasn't surrounded by ordinary criminals.

As you sit in the season of your prison experience, you may be tempted to ask, "How did I get here? What did I do wrong?" Can I tell you that it's not what you did wrong but what you did right! You resisted the temptation to give in and quit. You stayed true to your journey. You remained faithful to the dream even when it took you into uncomfortable places.

It is the plan of God to get you from one place to another; from preview to feature film. In order to get you there, He has to place you in the presence of people who see the potential in you and the gifts God has given you. He will take what looks like calamity to the natural eye and use it to advance you. He will make *"all things work together for good to those who love God, to those who are the called according to His purpose"* (Romans 8:28). You weren't called to your own purpose. You were called to His purpose and He will not allow one ounce of pain, one tear, or even one drop of sweat to be wasted. When He is with you, like He was with Joseph, you are set up to succeed. You will undoubtedly be placed in environments that you do not like, but make sure that the Lord is with you. He is your key to victory. Go where He says to go, and do what He says to do!

Recognizing God's presence with you will keep you from acting and reacting in your flesh. Knowing that He is with you on the job, will make the difficult employees more tolerable and you will be less likely to speak disrespectfully. Your employer will take note of your steady disposition, and you will climb the corporate ladder faster than those with more experience than you. You may not get along with a family member, but acknowledging that He is with you will enable you to walk in love at the next family dinner. Family members will not even know why they trust you as much as they do with personal matters, but it will be because they know that you walk in love and discretion and will not judge them. You cannot respond constructively to others without God being with you.

2. Your key to get out of prison is IN the prison.

> *"The supply is in your assignment."*
> STEVEN FURTICK

Joseph was serving his prison sentence out with two other individuals, a baker and a butler, who were not from his neck of the woods. Joseph was from Potiphar's house. Potiphar, who was under the King's authority, used his influence to place Joseph in a jail set aside for the King's prisoners. It's not clear exactly what the baker and the butler had done to offend the King and deserve prison, but there they were with Joseph. Joseph was now with people who at one point had direct access to the King. Not only was he in prison with these two, but also he was in charge of them. They answered to him. He was held accountable to be aware of all their actions, interactions, meals, and anything they did large and small.

With eyes wide open survey your environment. Who is near you? Who do you know that is connected to the one holding the keys to your release from the prison you are in? Potiphar put Joseph in prison, but the King had the authority to release him. Because of the nature of the offense, Potiphar could not let Joseph out. It was a personal offense against he and his wife. He couldn't risk his reputation by releasing Joseph, and because of this Joseph was destined to stay bound for the rest of his life unless a higher supremacy intervened.

Keep in mind that there will be times when, like with Joseph, the same person that listened to your accuser and put you in prison will not be the same person that vindicates you. Your vindication will come from someone in a greater place of authority, who also has the ability to alter the spectrum of your influence. Stop asking for solutions to your problems from the person that created your problem and realize that they no longer have the power to change anything for you.

As you await your release, get to know your elements. Know who has been placed near you. Your freedom from prison is connected to whom you are connected to. It's in who and what you have access to. Right now, in this very moment of immobility, God is moving to bring alignment for the dream to become a reality. The key to getting out of where you are and to the dream is not something that is beyond you. It is currently within your reach.

3. Be willing to help another dreamer.

> *"You have not lived today until you have done something for someone who can never repay you."*
> JOHN BUNYAN

> *"Helping one person may not change the world, but it could change the world for one person."*
> UNKNOWN

As you push closer and closer to the finish line, there will be opportunities presented for you to take your eyes off of your own journey to help someone else fulfill their dream. The greatest way to breathe life into your dream that seems to be asleep is to use your gifts to help someone else. What posture do you take when someone asks for help and it is in your power to help them? Are you willing to roll up your sleeves and say, "Nothing is happening in my world right now, let me help you with yours. What do you need me to do?"

A writer that hits writer's block feels alive and free when they take time out to edit someone else's work. Words start to flow, and ideas for their own book begin to take shape. Dancers who feel uninspired will suddenly gain creative inspiration as they help choreograph a fellow dancer's routine. Someone may be asked to serve as an assistant before their appointed time to be the boss. Your time of helping to serve someone else's dream may take longer than you anticipate, but it is time well spent. Whether it was a few weeks, months or even years, there is something in serving someone else's dream that helps to cultivate and develop your gift so that when it is time for you to launch, you are better prepared. Because while serving someone else's dream, you will gain greater insight and learn healthier ways to steward the dream that God has given you.

Joseph was not just a dreamer, but he was also a dreamer with a gift from God to interpret dreams. Your gifts and talents are bigger than just you. They are meant for a greater impact beyond your immediate circle and are to serve humanity. It is not meant for selfish gain alone but for the advancement of other people as well. There are God-given dreams locked up in the hearts and minds of those around you.

Joseph was incarcerated with the baker and the butler who, on the same night, had dreams. Both men were troubled by their dreams because they did not have an interpretation for them. Remember, it was a dream that got Joseph into this whole journey. But somewhere between his first dream and now, Joseph learned how to

Joseph took the gift of the dream that was given to him and learned how to use it to help other people!

interpret dreams. Joseph took the gift of the dream that was given to him and learned how to use it to help other people! It is often the struggle with the thing that you were first given that is the very key to your release. Instead of cursing it, wrestle with it. Wrestle with that "thing" until you learn how to "interpret" the thing.

God was with Joseph. Joseph says to them, *"Do not interpretations belong to God? Tell them to me please"* (Genesis 40:8b). Joseph was aware of who was with him, and because he knew who was with him, he trusted that God would empower him to use his gift to help someone else. In that moment he was not consumed by his circumstances. He was not fixated on what was or was not happening with his appeal for freedom or a plot of revenge. He was not sulking in a corner licking his wounds, crying about how unfairly he had been treated. Joseph, the dreamer, maximized his moment and stepped into destiny.

As you help others fulfill their dreams, be mindful to keep your heart in check. Give without any expectation to receive anything in return. Joseph interpreted the dreams of the baker and the butler without any strings attached. He told them that they would be released from prison in three days. Joseph asked the butler to remember him when he came before the king and to mention his case. Three days later they were released. One week went by, and then another week, and then a month went by, and then another. Joseph surely thought there would be movement in his case by now. But the butler did not mention him to the Pharaoh. Genesis 40:23 states that the butler "forgot him."

4. Patience is produced in prison.

"Patience is not the ability to wait, but the ability to keep a good attitude while waiting."
ANONYMOUS

Joseph remained in prison for another TWO years! This doesn't seem fair at all. Joseph was innocent of the allegations. What do you do when your hope and anticipation for release doesn't go as you planned? What do you do when God wants to orchestrate your liberation but His date is different than yours? You have to become even more patient. I think this is the hardest statement to hear when you have already been through "hell" and you just want it to be over. This level of patience will involve many days of questions without very many answers and you may even begin to question if the dream is worth it. If allowed, prison will try to choke out of you any remaining hope you have left. You will find yourself at a crossroads, and you will have to make a decision: continue on or give up?

There is nothing wrong with anticipating the next stage, wishing it would hurry up. But do not become so focused on what's next that you do not get everything you can get out of where you are. Every fifteen-year-old looks around the corner with so much excitement to the day they turn sixteen. They get to drive! There's a level of independence that comes with sixteen. They live in the moment for a few days and almost immediately they change their focus to turning eighteen where "true" independence comes, they get to go off to college, move out, and get to "do what they want." What they do not realize is that the TWO years between sixteen and eighteen are to prepare them to move out, to make decisions on their own that will not destroy their life, but enhance their experience at the next level. Those TWO years may seem long but a lot is being accomplished in them.

"When there is no way out, you find a deeper way in."
CASSIAN SKARSSEN
(FICTIONAL MOVIE CHARACTER)

I greatly enjoy watching movies. But I don't do scary or horror movies because I will not pay for what God said He didn't give me, which is a *"spirit of fear"* (2 Timothy 1:7). Going to the theater is my escape from my day-to-day responsibilities. It gives me an opportunity to laugh, think, reflect, and be entertained. I often said that if I wasn't in full-time ministry that I would have become a food and movie critic. Most of my favorite movies are action based, and the dialogue doesn't require the depth of a Shakespearian production. But every now and then I will come across a line from a movie, which for some reason, will stick with me. The aforementioned quote was one of those lines. There will be times in life where there appears to be no way out, but the actual way out is to go further in. If God is not allowing a release from the circumstance, it is because there are things still yet to learn. Consequently, since we can't get out, we must go deeper into God. These are the times to dig your heels in deeper and remain resolute that God knows what He is doing even though the pain of the moment seems unbearable.

Undoubtedly this extended stint in confinement gives Joseph additional time to deal with deeply uncomfortable emotional matters. And one of the many emotions Joseph may have had to deal with is the theme of rejection. You see, once again, Joseph has been rejected. Rejection has been a theme in Joseph's life. He must have felt rejected by his brothers (family), rejected by Potiphar (employer), rejected by Potiphar's wife (associate), and now rejected by the butler

The closing of a door by God is not rejection of you but rather protection for you.

(friend). As with Joseph, we must not allow the rejection of others to equate rejection by God. The closing of a door by God is not rejection of you but rather protection for you. God's timing is perfect even though the moment feels imperfect. People may reject and forget you but you are always on God's mind!

It is important to get healed while you are isolated with God. Don't reject the "backside of the mountain" experience as useless time. This is time to go in further with God and to make sure you are healed and whole. You cannot allow the scars of the journey to cause you to emotionally dismantle all the gains from the previous stages. Take this time to work on you and be transparent with God. There is nothing more dangerous than an unhealthy leader who has influence with people.

How you come out of a situation is reflective of if you stayed in it long enough. When the timer goes off and you pull the cake out of the oven, the expectation is that the cake is fully risen and ready to be served. If the cake is flat or the batter is still wet, it is an indication that the cake was pulled out too early and needs more time in the oven (hot, confined space) in order to fully cook so that it can be served. You cannot shorten or speed up the oven time. There is value in staying in the crucible of your predicament and letting God bring you out when it is time!

Opportunity Knocks When You Least Expect It

"When one door closes another opens. But often we look so long so regretfully upon the closed door that we fail to see the one that has opened for us."
HELEN KELLER

As Joseph waited in jail for two years, doubt of his release probably began to settle in. He possibly began to settle into the idea of being in prison forever. And yet I believe that Joseph never fully gave up hope. The reason for this belief is because the story didn't end in the jail. The only way to survive that level of disappointment is to recall what God has promised and to remember how

God delivered before. Joseph recalled that God remembered him in the pit and delivered him. He replayed all the times in Potiphar's house where he was shown favor and was promoted. He counted his blessings and saw how even in his current prison he had found favor again and was promoted. Joseph remembered God's goodness throughout his life, especially in the dark places, and I believe this is what fueled Joseph to continue on. God did not bring you this far to fail you. Hold on with everything you have! The end of this stage is within sight!! Borrowing the words from one of my favorite Tye Tribbett songs, "If He did it before, He will do it again…"

An opportunity arose for Joseph to interpret another dream. This time it was the Pharaoh's dream. When no one else could interpret his dream, the butler remembered Joseph, and recommended him to the Pharaoh.

"A man's gift makes room for him and brings him before great men"
PROVERBS 18:16

Do not be discouraged by the time that it takes for people to recognize the gifts that you have inside of you. Even in the midst of what seems like an eternity of waiting, you are being developed. When it seems like all hope is lost and everyone has forgotten about you, remember that God has a plan. The butler forgot Joseph. But God did not forget Joseph. He used the gift that he gave Joseph to bring him before Pharaoh. Pharaoh had a dream that no one could interpret.

"Then it came to pass, at the end of two years, that Pharaoh had a dream…And Pharaoh told them his dreams, but there was no one who could interpret them for Pharaoh."
Genesis 41:1a, 8b

The Lord interrupted Pharaoh's sleep to set Joseph up for freedom. When it's time for your release, God will trouble the sleep of the most powerful person on earth in order to get you free. When it's time, it's time and no one can stop it! When God sets up an appointment for you to collide with destiny, no man can sleep on it.

It will become clear to all that you are the only person for the job. No one can take the company to the next level like you, and no one can handle the team better than you. When everyone is befuddled because they cannot figure out what to do next, someone will remember how you helped them with their dream in past seasons and your name will be mentioned. All you have to do is be faithful and show up when called. Joseph was ready when they told him that Pharaoh was requesting his presence. He didn't have to collect his things. He didn't have to gather his thoughts. He was ready.

The way you become prepared is by working on the things you can control and not being consumed by the things that are out of your control. This is the beauty of the prison stage. You have to work on you. Your dream may be to buy a house, so work on your financial discipline and save your money. Your dream may be to buy a car, so work on paying your bills on time so when you qualify you won't have to pay for a car that is double the cost because your financing can only be approved at 24% interest. Maybe your dream is to be married, so take this time to work on your emotions, love capacity, and negotiating skills. Or maybe your dream is to open a business, so you should definitely use this time to read books on successful businesses and why others fail. If you want to be a physical trainer, work on your health first. Consider practicing, studying, lifting, reading, learning, listening, mentoring, etc. while no one is looking so you will be prepared when everyone is looking. Preparation time is never wasted time. Use this time to prepare yourself for the opportunity that is coming. There is no time to get ready when your number is called…you must be ready!

"Success occurs when opportunity meets preparation."
ZIG ZIGLAR

Pharaoh made the request, and they *"brought him quickly out of the dungeon; and he shaved, changed his clothing, and came to Pharaoh"* (Genesis 41:14). All Joseph had to do was make himself presentable. He already had everything else he needed inside of him to stand before the one who could change the trajectory of the rest of his life with one word. Don't waste time on only being outwardly prepared while neglecting the importance of being inwardly ready. There is nothing worse than an empty pretty box.

There is nothing worse than an empty pretty box.

Joseph's prison produced patience in him. He waited for his turn. He helped where he could when he could. He didn't give in when things got difficult. He remained steady and consistent. He didn't try to force the shift in season by telling everyone that he was the one who interpreted the dreams of the baker and the butler that preceded their release. He didn't brag about his gifts. He remained silent and let his reputation speak for itself when it was time. He had gained a reputation from the time he entered Potiphar's house to the time he was called by Pharaoh. His reputation of consistency, integrity, reliability, dependability, and accuracy in gifting preceded him. He was known for being steady in the midst of hardship. Joseph did not build a reputation of fighting or being contentious. He didn't have a bad attitude, and he wasn't unpleasant to be around. Joseph surrendered to the process and used it as an opportunity to grow. How will you choose to wait? What reputation are you building? Will you be ready when you are called?

"As I walked out the door toward the gate that would lead to my freedom, I knew if I didn't leave my bitterness and hatred behind, I'd still be in prison."

NELSON MANDELA

Eyes Wide Open

When Joseph was presented to Pharaoh, Pharaoh made a statement. Not a question, but a statement based on the reputation that Joseph had acquired, saying, *"I have heard it said of you that you can understand a dream, to interpret it"* (Genesis 41:15). People were talking about the things Joseph had accomplished and how he handled himself. His name was being mentioned in circles that he was not engaged in yet. Just like Joseph, your reputation and conduct will precede you and people will make mention of your name. They will brag about you and your gifts. They will want to be associated with you and will "name drop" your name in elite circles in hopes to remain connected once you enter the group, but no matter what their motives for mentioning you are, it is your gifts and talents that got you there. You earned your seat at the table. Glory be to God!

Joseph's response to Pharaoh's statement was, *"It is not in me; God will give Pharaoh an answer of peace"* (Genesis 41:16). Joseph was well aware of the source and dependency of the Dream Giver to give him the interpretation. He trusted that what had been cultivated in him in the prison would be proven once again. Joseph's journey produced a trust in him concerning God that no one could shake or intimidate. Joseph trusted God!

When people point to you as the source of your accomplishments, you point to God. It is only by the empowering of the Lord in each season of testing and trial that you are able to answer Pharaoh's request when called out of the dungeon. Everything in Joseph's life up to this point was leading to this moment. Because of every stage in Joseph's journey, he was able to approach this situation with eyes wide open. I don't know if you have ever experienced this, but it is like the moment when everything slows down and you are able to see everything clearly. You are in the moment and above it at the same time. You know exactly what to do because this is the moment that the realization of your dream has been waiting on. Everything has led to this. And it is from the depth of this well of experience that Joseph was able to speak.

Then Joseph said to the Pharaoh, "The dreams of Pharaoh are..." "... let Pharaoh select..." "Let Pharaoh do this..." So the advice was good in the eyes of Pharaoh and in the eyes of all his servants.
Genesis 41:25, 33, 34, 37

Chapter 4 Reflections

"Still, I rise."
MAYA ANGELOU

Meditate on these scripture verses:

Proverbs 3:5-6, Proverbs 18:16, Genesis 41

Reflect:

- It is easy to pinpoint a God dream because the dream is more about others than it is about yourself.

- Remember that the devil cannot stop the dream, but he will try and break the heart that the dream has to come through.

- Joseph took the gift of the dream that was given to him and learned how to use it to help other people.

- The closing of a door by God is not the rejection of you but rather protection for you.

Questions:

What does freedom look like for you? Have you ever felt forgotten, left behind, or insignificant? Are you prepared for the opportunity that is getting ready to knock or will you miss it do to self-loathing?

_____
_____
_____
_____
_____
_____
_____

Prayer:

"Journal a prayer of faith that is personal and vulnerable, asking God to turn on the light in your heart. Thank Him that He is not hiding Himself from you but, rather, is opening your eyes to trust in Jesus." – Aaron Dailey

---

Activity:

Make a list of the books or articles you can read that can help you get better prepared during this season of confinement. Preparation is not wasted time. Also, make a list of the top 3 things you can do that will aide in the development of your dream. And then begin doing them!

5

THE PROMISE

*"Someone took that same situation
you've been complaining about and won with it."*
UNKNOWN

Every dream has a promise tied to it. The reason we pursue the dream
is because of the promise that is waiting for us at the finish line. You
have made it past the jealousy and harsh accusations of your critics.
You have been mishandled, underappreciated, judged, discounted,
devalued, and hated. You have been put in a pit and isolated by
those who by nature and proximity should have protected you, and
then you were taken out of that very pit and sold into slavery by the
same people. In spite of your circumstances, you managed to remain
humble, steady, consistent, and faithful to your assignment. When
things were hard, you trusted God. When you found favor and promotion, you still trusted God. In the face of increased adversity and
mounting lies resulting in further persecution, you believed God.
Your faith in Him and His ability to keep you through it all, mold
you, shape you, and create something out of nothing never wavered.
You fought not to create a habitat of bitterness in your heart. You
stayed pliable and teachable. You've lost everything, gotten it back,
and lost it again. There were days when you felt like you took two
steps forward and one step back, questioning if you were making any
progress at all. But you didn't give up! You kept taking the two steps
and learned what it meant to push through and be pushed back. You
used your time wisely, learning from your mistakes and studying

to perfect your craft. You resisted the urge to make things happen for yourself; creating "opportunities" for yourself. You declined the shortcuts in order to gain all of the wisdom that you could get out of the pit, Potiphar's house, and the prison. You didn't compromise or lower your standards but trusted that God would be faithful to every promise that He made to you concerning your life, your dream, and everyone connected to you.

Don't devalue or underestimate what you have accomplished thus far. Let's reflect on the victories up to this point:

- You wrote the vision, made it plain and waited for someone to pick it up and run with it | Habakkuk 2:2
- You believed that He is faithful to all His promises | Psalm 145:13
- You trusted that all His promises are "Yes" and "amen" | 2 Corinthians 1:20
- You were resolved that "though the dream lingered, if you would just wait on it, it would certainly come and not delay" | Habakkuk 2:3

When it didn't seem as if your dream would ever get off the ground, you stepped outside of your box to help someone make their dreams come true. You encouraged others when no one encouraged you. You treated others how you so wished someone would treat you. You dreamed with others when no one dreamed with you. You spent time in research and development for others' projects when no one wanted to put in any time or energy into your dream. You sowed financial seeds into helping others get their projects off the ground when no one wanted to open their wallets to you. All of the lessons you learned from the pit, at Potiphar's house, and in prison were made available to make someone else's dream a reality while your dream laid dormant. You watched as other people dreamed a dream, executed said dream, and lived their dream. But you didn't complain about how long your season of brainstorming, fundraising, writing, planning, meeting, or idea pitching took. You committed to each step as it arrived and for however long it took. You learned the lessons as they came, learned how to troubleshoot problems, and corrected errors.

All of these stages and phases were used in order to get you to this moment right here. It was to prepare you to be able to handle the success of the next stage without pride and ego getting in the way. God used every ounce of pain to thicken your skin as He tended to your heart to make it soft and empathetic. He used the "No's" to help you appreciate the "Yes's." He taught you how to take care of and be a good steward over the "little" so that when it is time for abundance you would know how to take care of it responsibly. Learning to take care of someone else's property (an apartment) then transitioning that care into your home ownership. Living from paycheck to paycheck to having multiple savings accounts. Learning to be grateful for public transportation to owning your own car and being gracious enough to give someone else a ride. Appreciating the lessons gained from baking in your cramped kitchen to now baking in a brick-and-mortar shop. Everything that you have gone through and endured was not just about you getting to the finish line. The major point of concern was your sustainability once you got to the finish line. The question at the end of the pit, Potiphar's house, and the prison is "will you be able to maintain the promise once you get it or will the position and power corrupt you?"

"A corrupt heart will never handle a position of power well."
BRANDIE MANIGAULT

It's been said that opportunity knocks at the door, and if you are not ready you will miss it. But you will not miss this chance if you take advantage of every opportunity to learn, grow, and develop. And NOW that you are ready, it is time to step in to the promise of the dream you saw before the journey began. The moment that you have been waiting for is now upon you. What will you do? Walk through that door in full confidence knowing that you are ready for it!

Stage Lessons

"So many of our dreams at first seem impossible, then they seem improbable, and then, when we summon the will, they soon become inevitable."

CHRISTOPHER REEVE

1. The place that bound you is often the very place that you will have dominion over.

Joseph was a slave in the palace, but within a few moments of each other, he was put in a position, that with the exception of Pharaoh, no one in Egypt would have more authority than him. Joseph, the man that was accused of being inappropriate with the wife of a prominent official, was placed in authority under the blessing of the highest-ranking member of society. The stain of his reputation (disowned and estranged from his family, accused rapist, felon, slave) was a non-issue in the eyes of the King. Joseph was not just given power, but he was given great influence. This is what Pharaoh said to Joseph…

"You shall be over my house, and all my people shall be ruled according to your word; only in regard to the throne will I be greater than you…See I have set you over all the land of Egypt"

GENESIS 41:40-41

In receiving power from Pharaoh, he subsequently gained power of Potiphar's house, the house that he was a slave in, rose to power in, and was banished from for a crime he didn't commit. When it's time for you to rise and stand in your gift, you will find that the people that tried to hold you back with their words and accusations will ultimately be placed under the submission of your gifting, and whether forced or of their own volition will give you due respect and respond appropriately. God has a way of making those who do you wrong be the same ones that have to make it right and will at some point eventually need you. This paradigm is found throughout the Bible, but here is an example from Paul's life…

> *But Paul said to them, "They have beaten us openly, uncon-*
> *demned Romans, and have thrown us into prison. And now do they*
> *put us out secretly? No indeed! Let them come themselves and get us*
> *out." And the officers told these words to the magistrates, and they*
> *were afraid when they heard that they were Romans. Then they came*
> *and pleaded with them and brought them out, and asked them to*
> *depart from the city.*
>
> ### ACTS 16:37-39

I personally believe the proverbial prison stage is a critical experience. It is necessary because it purges our personal agendas and provides space and time to receive healing because of the forgiveness we choose to give to others. The length of stay is correlated to the amount of time it takes for us to be humbled so that when we stand in the realization of the dream we are more purposeful and grateful to God. Subsequently we won't waste time with wanting vindication from those who had a hand in putting us in the pit and in prison, because this course of response will only jeopardize the length of stay in the dream that we so patiently waited for.

2. Recognize and value the process.

God prepares you at every level for the next level. Understand that everything that you go through. Every good moment and every moment of hardship is for you to learn from and glean all that you can to take to the next phase.

As a boy, Joseph's father entrusted him with age-appropriate tasks designed to set him up for his next level. He tended the sheep. Tending sheep was not just sitting on a hill watching them all day. Joseph had to ensure the health and protection of the sheep by keeping a watchful eye out for predators, making sure they were fed, and leading them to waters to drink. It was not a passive assignment. At the age of seventeen Joseph learned responsibility for what was placed in his hands. He learned to be a servant leader, submitting to the direction and order of authority while being in authority himself. He put into effect everything he learned along the way so that he could maximize his current space.

Take note that you will be given the opportunity to lead while being led. You will find yourself being promoted on the job, second in command to the founder and CEO, but do not make the mistake of thinking or responding to your boss as if your authority supersedes theirs. Joseph used his experience from the fields at his father's house and built on it in Potiphar's house. He took the knowledge he gained in Potiphar's house and implemented and built on it in the prison. Now when presented with the opportunity to run Egypt, he was fully equipped to live out the dream he saw while tending sheep as a boy.

Remember, faithfulness is the key to seeing your dream come true. Be faithful to yourself, not compromising in who you are. Joseph was a shepherd. He remained true to who he was as he progressed up the ranks. He was faithful to his training. He didn't abandon his teaching along the way. As the responsibilities increased, he grew in his knowledge, but it was built upon the previous training.

3. Hold on to your dreams even if it takes longer than you anticipated.

Joseph was 17 when the dream started burning in his heart. He wasn't looking to do more than be a good son, and work for his dad, but the dream came and he couldn't let it go.

Joseph was 30 years old when his dream finally became a reality. It took 13 years for Joseph to see the manifestation of everything. Even though it took longer than he planned he held the dream tight. He didn't abandon it when things looked contrary to what he expected it to look like.

Any dream worth having is worth waiting on. Stay fully committed through the different stages. It's in the process that you prove your merit to God, that you are worthy to carry the dream. Will you see it through until the end? Are you capable of handling it when it comes? Are you willing to pay the price for it?

It takes a long time to go through school before the university will issue you a degree. Why is it that you have to carry general education classes along with your core courses? Why is it that you have to take a test before you can pass each class and move on to the next one? It is to prove your ability to handle the information and apply the information properly when the time comes. It is to make sure that you can take what you have learned through rigorous testing and be able to apply it in real-world situations. The academic experience is an incubator to prepare you for real-world conditions that will not be as accommodating and hospitable to you as school was. Learn the lesson, pass the test, graduate, and glide across the stage going from student to practitioner.

4. Refuse to let offense stop you.

I am reminded of an old adage that says, "It's common for the dog to bark at the moon, but if the moon barks back, the dog becomes famous." You are the polarizing attraction that will always provoke barking. Just remember to not respond negatively because moons are incapable of barking.

One of the greatest things that will distract you and keep you in a cycle of waiting unnecessarily is carrying offense. Joseph could have remained offended at his brothers. He could have been offended and let resentment and bitterness take root in his heart as a result of how Potiphar's wife's accusations set off a chain reaction beginning with his stay in prison. And he could have easily held on to bitterness at the butler that forgot about him after he helped him. No man's lack of support, lack of encouragement, or attempted sabotage is worth you compromising your values by holding on to offense. You have put in the time, work, and energy to get to where you are, and it would be a waste of time if you allowed offense to be the reason that the dream is further delayed.

You are the only one responsible for your reactions and responses to other people. They can do what they do, but it is how you choose to react that counts. Will you allow them to get you out of character or will you use their behavior as a tool to sharpen your dutiful position? Do not lower your standards. Demand that they come higher to meet the bar that you have set for yourself.

"When they go low, we go high."
MICHELLE OBAMA

Mercy Me

"You will achieve more in this world through acts of mercy than you will through acts of retribution."
NELSON MANDELA

There will come a point when those who doubted your dream will come face to face with it. Joseph's brothers had that moment when famine hit the land and they were forced to reach out to Egypt for help.

"And Joseph said to his brothers, 'Please come near to me…I am Joseph your brother, whom you sold into slavery into Egypt. But now, do not therefore be grieved or angry with yourselves because you sold me here; for God sent me before you to preserve your life…And God sent me before you to preserve a posterity for you in the earth, and to save your lives by a great deliverance…and He has made me a father to Pharaoh, and lord of all his house, and a ruler throughout all the land of Egypt.'"
Genesis 45:4-7

Joseph's brothers thought that they had gotten rid of Joseph years earlier. They assumed that because of their actions that Joseph would never be anything and that they had succeeded in ruining the chances of his dream ever coming true. What shock and awe they must have felt when they found themselves at the mercy of their brother, the dreamer. Those with no dreams will always have to answer to those who fulfill their dreams. Joseph's brothers now find themselves in front of the very one they despised and tried to destroy. Can you image the terror that flooded their hearts?! In this climactic moment, Joseph has a choice to make: succumb to the emotion of revenge or stand in the transforming power of the last THIRTEEN years and choose to forgive and let it go!

What will your response be when the ones who doubted you are now in front of you and need your help? Will you make them pay for what they did to you? Now that you have the power, will you withhold goodness? Or will you extend to them the grace and **You will discover true strength if you decide to exercise restraint.** mercy that you wish they had given you? You will discover true strength if you decide to exercise restraint. Because your strength is in your restraint.

Joseph was true to what had been cultivated in him throughout the different seasons of his life. He choose to be loving and called them in close and told them to bring his father, his younger brother, and his whole household to him. There will be people, like Joseph's father, who will not know what happened to you and have assumed the worst because of what someone else has said about you. But finally they will be presented with the opportunity to see for themselves the fulfillment of your dream.

"It's hard for people to celebrate where you are if they don't know where you've been because we tend to view people through our history instead of theirs."
KRIS VALLOTON

It will be difficult for people to believe that you are not the person that they expected you to be based upon how they treated you. The change may take time for people to embrace. The new you, the evolved you, will baffle people, but do not let their doubt cause you to back down. Stand confident in who you are and wait for your consistent behavior to prove that you are who you say you are.

Joseph would have been well within his newfound authority to afford his brothers the same pit and prison that was given to him by their actions. But because of Joseph's mercy it provided a greater favor for his family than even what Joseph had calculated. Joseph said to them...

"You shall dwell in the land of Goshen, and you shall be near to me, you and your children... There I will provide for you."
GENESIS 45:10-11A

Believe it or not, but the outcome and well-being of those who mistreated you is cocooned in your ability to forgive them and show them mercy. When Pharaoh heard that Joseph's family was in town, it "pleased" him, and he said...

"do not be concerned about your goods, for the best of the land of Egypt is yours."
GENESIS 45:20

And upon their arrival the Pharaoh tells Joseph...

"if you know any competent men among them make them chief herdsmen over my livestock."
GENESIS 47:6

This is so amazing that it is worth saying again! The comfort and prosperity of those that rejected you is contingent upon your forgiveness of them!

But even after benefiting from your promotions in life, there will still be doubt in the hearts of those who have done you wrong. They may still not believe that you are genuine in your response to their presence. Though you have loved them and embraced them, they still carry the guilt of their past actions toward you.

> *"Perhaps Joseph will hate us, and may actually repay us for all the evil which we did to him."*
> **Genesis 50:15**

The brothers felt that as long as Jacob, their father, was alive that Joseph wouldn't bring that grief to his father by killing his sons. But now that Jacob has died, they feel that they are no longer safe and will soon experience Joseph's wrath. But Joseph's heart was tender to them in spite of all that he had experienced at their initiation. Joseph's response was…

> *"Do not be afraid, for am I in the place of God…do not be afraid; I will provide for you and your little ones." And he comforted them and spoke kindly to them.*
> **Genesis 50:19, 21**

Like Joseph, you must have a kind word ready for them. It's amazing how much Joseph had grown in this journey and the type of person he became. Remember, earlier in Joseph's life his brothers couldn't speak a kind word to him (Genesis 37:4) and now Joseph is giving to them, in the moment they needed it the most, the thing that they didn't give to him, in the moment he needed it the most. The journey of the pursuit of the dream that God gives you will change you in ways that you didn't know were possible or even needed. The journey of the stages prepares you for the promise of the dream.

Bad Intentions

"Courage is the most important of all the virtues because without courage, you can't practice any other virtue consistently."
MAYA ANGELOU

Courage is the raincoat that every dreamer must wear when the onslaught of malcontent begins to rain down. Try as you might to please everyone and be nice to those around you, there will still be those who wish you harm because of where they are. You must remember that their intentions for you are not about you and in most cases is a result of them projecting upon you the unhappiness that they are experiencing because of their lack of courage to pursue their dream as you have.

"But as for you, ye thought evil against me; but God meant it unto good, to bring to pass, as it is this day, to save much people alive."
Genesis 50:20

I find this statement by Joseph to his brothers to be another indicator of the growth that he experienced as a result of his journey. Because of the process, Joseph realized something that his brothers would never understand. God used their betrayal to be a catalyst for great change. For at this very moment in time, Joseph's brothers have a front-row seat to witness how God used Joseph, now the Governor of Egypt, to give wisdom and insight to the Pharaoh that helped to save the lives of millions of people during this unprecedented time. It was Joseph's policies that procured food initiatives that ensured there would be enough food to sustain the people through seven years of famine. It is at this very moment that Joseph's brothers, with tears in their eyes and regret in their hearts, realize that all of Joseph's dreams from 13 years ago were truly God-given because they were participating and standing in one of the very scenes he had described to them.

In most cases you can't control people's intentions regarding you, whether good or bad. But what you can control is how you to respond to them. When you begin to understand that even though people may have meant evil towards you, God has a way of taking their bad intentions and using those moments as paradigm shifts in your story. Remember, without the bad intentions of the brothers throwing Joseph into that pit, he never would have made it to Potiphar's house, and that house was the beginning of his journey in Egypt that would eventually lead him to the place of influence and power that he eventually held. When you fully embrace that bad intentions from people, even loved ones, is sometimes necessary, you will instead want to shake their hand and tell them, "Thank you for not believing in me and betraying me."

God can use every "No," rejection, and betrayal as a catalyst that will catapult you to the place those same actors never thought was possible. The intriguing thing is that in most cases these launchings serve to position you to be a help to a lot of people. So, when people with bad intentions show themselves, just look beyond them to the multitudes of people that you are being positioned to help. Take courage, love those that mean you harm and watch how in time God will have used their actions to strategically position you in your dreams.

Buried in the Dream

"In the end, it's not the years in your life that count. It's the life in your years."
ABRAHAM LINCOLN

You will prosper beyond what you thought was possible at the onset of your dream. The dream wasn't given to you to torment you or to tease you. And it wasn't given to you to afflict others. It was given to you in order to show you what is possible, what is attainable, and what you can have. Joseph started with a flock of sheep at 17, and when he died at 110 years of age he was ruler over all of Egypt. Even though the process for the dream took 13 years of waiting and development, it pales in comparison to the time he was able to live IN the dream. Joseph was able to live in the dream, as the second most powerful man in Egypt next to Pharaoh, for 80 years! He was able to provide counsel and help give direction to a nation for 80 years!! He was able to provide for his family for 80 years!!! The length of time Joseph lived out his dream was longer than most peoples lifetimes.

As you remain faithful in your stewardship of the dream and the people attached to it, you will see the dream increase and expand beyond what you would have imagined when the dream first entered your heart. That's why it is very important that you don't allow people to interpret your dream. People only have the capacity to see your dream from their vantage point, and if it doesn't favor them they will frown on it. Joseph saw this day of ruling, but all that his family could see was them bowing. If Joseph had decided to stop pursuing the dream, then who knows what the finale of their whole family would have looked like in the face of the impending famine. You, and your dream, could be the salvation for your entire family!

Joseph was buried after he saw success and the totality of the dream. He lived the dream. He didn't die with the dream still in his heart. At the end of your life, will your dream still be in your mind or will your dream be seen in the earth and benefiting the lives of others? Will your influence be felt and experienced, or will we be void of your life's work and contribution? I don't know about you, but when my days are concluded I, just like Joseph, want to be buried in the land that is the result of the dream. I don't want to take the dream with me, but I want to get out of me every book, message, session, and word that God has placed in me. Don't die with the dream…die IN the dream!

So as I close the chapter on this portion of my dream, please allow me to encourage you and tell you from a place of achievement that the dream is possible. You are reading "a dream." You are physically holding a dream in your hand. And if God can do it for me and through me, then He very well can do the same thing for you. I am the least likely author, but I am the most vivid dreamer. I'm not living to prove anyone wrong but rather I live to prove God right; He was right to entrust me to live out His dream in me. So I want to encourage you to wipe the tears from your eyes and get a renewed vision for your dream. Go get your dream out of the closet and knock the dust off of it! Work the dream. Maximize the dream. Live the dream. Die in the dream. Be buried in the dream!

> *"The size of your dreams must always exceed your current capacity to achieve them."*
> ELLEN JOHNSON SIRLEAF
> NOBEL PEACE PRIZE WINNER AND 24TH PRESIDENT OF LIBERIA

Chapter 5 Reflections

*"Someone took that same situation
you've been complaining about and won with it."*
UNKNOWN

Meditate on these scripture verses:

Genesis 41:40-41, Acts 16:37-39, Genesis 45

Reflect:

- You will discover true strength if you decide to exercise restraint.

- Be buried in the dream.

- Every dream has a promise tied to it.

- "So many of our dreams at first seem impossible, then they seem improbable, and then, when we summon the will, they soon become inevitable." – Christopher Reeve (Superman)

Questions:

What are the stage lessons? Which one of the stage lessons resonates with you the most and why? What is the promise of your dream?

_____

_____

_____

_____

_____

_____

_____

_____

Prayer:

"Father thank you for reminding that my dream is really your dream because it started with you. And consequently, the fulfillment of this dream is one in which it is serving people. Help me to always remember that any blessing you give me is not just about me but about others as well. Let me have a heart for people and see all people as you see them. Help me to love them like you love them. Help me to use the promise of this dream to be an expression and extension of your love for mankind. It is in that space that you are well pleased. In Jesus name. Amen."

Activity:

Envision yourself in the place of your promise. This time envision the people around you. Who are they? What do they look like? What are the demographics, generational and social-economic make-up of the people that your dream is serving? Now begin to list how your dream serves them. If you have trouble seeing this then go back to the prayer in this section and continue to pray it until it is in your heart and then transfer it to paper. Let this list be a guiding principle as you serve humanity from the place of promise.

_____

_____

_____

_____

_____

_____

_____

_____

_____

_____

_____

_____

_____

6

DREAM AGAIN

*"The path from dreams to success does exist. May you have the vision
to find it, the courage to get on to it, and the perseverance to follow it."*
KALPANA CHAWLA

Are you ready to dream…are you ready to dream again? The dream
given to you is not dead. It is not forgotten. It is living, and all it
needs is for you to believe in it again.

As a dreamer you carry something that is specifically designed
with you in mind. God has taken into consideration and accounted
for your abilities and inabilities, your skill set, your resources, support base, your connections, and He tailored a dream to fit those
guidelines. He also took into account that you would recognize your
need for Him to fill in every deficiency you have. He knew that you
would ultimately lean more on Him than yourself, resources, and
community, thus making you the perfect candidate to be a dreamer.

God-given dreams are often given to trailblazers; those who
can handle the pressures of oncoming scrutiny for a new idea, the
challenges of setbacks, and the strength to stand for what they
believe in. They are given to individuals who don't mind being alone
for a season, unique, different from the status quo. Dreams are given
to people who are not just starters but finishers because they see it
through until the end.

A potential challenge for a trailblazer is that you will find it difficult for someone to help you with your dream due to the fact that

what you dream has only been seen in the eyes of God and the eyes of your heart. No one will understand the scope or the magnitude of what it will take to get that business off of the ground except you and God. Individuals will only be able to help in limited capacities at different stages of execution. The vision of the blueprints for your niche sub shop, or youth center, or after-school program, or financial consulting firm will look different than the blueprints of someone with the same general idea. You may both desire to become motivational speakers, but your focus may be trauma victims while your neighbor speaks to the hearts of young leaders. You share the same concepts, and may even be able to share some resources helping each other along the way; however, your dream will have your voice attached to it and your heartbeat thumping throughout it.

Along the journey from visualizing to actualizing, you will go through multiple stages and phases designed to build on each other. Your experiences are not meant to stand alone. They work together to build the "big picture." Like Legos, each "no" builds on your tenacity and strength. Each "yes" builds on your confidence. With every setback, you are adding another block of perseverance, and with every breakthrough you are adding another brick of victory. Your dream is a collective of every experience. They are not isolated incidents that do not affect anything else. What you deal with, overcome, power through, and triumph over today shapes the way you deal with, overcome, power through, and triumph over tomorrow. Learning how to deal with disappointment is equally as important as learning how to deal with accomplishment. In order to handle the dream in its totality (the power, the influence, the impact), you have to reach a level of maturity and integrity that comes as a product of each building block being placed on top of each other. Handling the dream with integrity and confidence, but with a lack of proper stewardship, will lead to a short-lived dream. Likewise, knowing how to steward what's in your hand but not having the confidence to do it, will cause an unhealthy

> **Your dream is a collective of every experience.**

dependence on others to steer the direction of the dream given to you. These are the building blocks of development that equip you to be well rounded and able to properly manage each aspect of the dream.

"Consider it pure joy, my brothers and sisters, whenever you face trials of many kinds, because you know that the testing of your faith produces perseverance. Let perseverance finish its work so that you may be mature and complete, not lacking anything."
James 1:2-4 NIV

Excuses, Excuses

"Ninety-nine percent of the failures come from people who have the habit of making excuses."
Dr. George Washington Carver

George Washington Carver was a black man in the Deep South. George was born with valid systematical excuses of a region, environment, and country that were against his very existence, let alone any success. But George refused to allow the excuses of segregation to become an impediment to the dreams God was giving him. He could have rightly cowered and hid behind the excuses, but rather he chose to stand and he became an agricultural scientist. Dr. Carver would later go on to say that when he went into the laboratory that it was as if, "God would take him behind the veil of a curtain and unveil to him the secrets of the peanut." Dr. Carver is famously known for creating peanut butter, but he is also entirely responsible for the creation of 145 peanut products along with numerous patents. He promoted the rotation of alternative crops to cotton, such as peanuts and sweet potatoes, to help prevent soil depletion and provide a source of food and improved quality of life for poor farmers. James Saxon Childers wrote, "Carver and his peanut products were almost solely responsible for the rise in the U.S. peanut production after the boll weevil devastated the American cotton crop beginning about 1892". Dr. Carver's inventions helped to save the economy of the South, even though he was never really properly lauded for such accomplishments because of his race. But he didn't allow the bitterness to rise to such a level that it would stop him from being a benefit to HUMANITY. Sometimes to pursue a dream you have to look past excuses (and people) and look to the greater good.

We can all make excuses because we all have them. Some excuses are valid and substantial, while others are convenient and unessential. But we must begin to look at excuses as opportunities to overcome challenges, thus making the fulfillment of the dream that much more satisfying. Overcoming excuses adds to the fabric of the backdrop of our story.

"He that is good for making excuses is seldom good for anything else."
Benjamin Franklin

Excuses are defined as, "a reason or explanation put forward to defend or justify a fault," and they are the things we use to remove ourselves from contention. We believe that because of them that we are not good enough or qualified enough. Our excuses can range from ethnicity, to lack of money or education, to gender bias, to not being born on the right side of the tracks, to mental or physical disability, to stature, or to a plethora of other things. The excuses become engrained within our psyches and consequently create a pseudo you that is incapable of completing new things. We become paralyzed and stuck in the mediocrity of the moment. We unknowingly submit to being fully consumed by the gripping fear of inadequacy.

But the truth of it all is that with God your "excuse" actually qualifies you...it is exactly what He has been looking for. In 1 Corinthians 1:27 it says, *"But God has chosen the foolish things of the world to put to shame the wise, and God has chosen the weak things of the world to put to shame the things which are mighty; and the base things of the world and the things which are despised God has chosen, and the things which are not, to bring to nothing the things that are, that no flesh should glory in His presence."* You don't realize it, but God has CHOSEN to use you BECAUSE of the excuse! God is not looking for a perfect unblemished person to be the curator of His dream. He prefers those who have excuses because who better to identify with people with excuses than people that have their own excuses. God will use you despite and sometimes because of, your perceived shortcomings.

I know this fact may be hard to believe because you have been told otherwise your entire life but let's look to the scriptures for actual empirical historical data of how God utilized flawed imperfect people with excuses to get a dream realized: Jacob (Israel's Patriarch) was a cheater, Peter (Apostle) cussed at a young girl and cut a man's ear off, David (King) had an affair, Noah (Patriarch) got drunk, Jonah (Prophet) ran from God, Paul (Apostle and writer of nearly two-thirds of the New Testament) was a murderer, Gideon (Judge) was insecure, Miriam (sister of Moses) was a gossip, Thomas (Disciple) was a doubter, Sara (Matriarch) was impatient, Elijah (Prophet) was moody, Moses (Deliverer of Israel) stuttered, Zaccheus (business man) was short, Abraham (Patriarch) was old, and Mary (Jesus's mother) was scared.

And God used it all! No more excuses!!

It's Not Too Late...

"You are never too old to set another goal or to dream a new dream."
C.S. Lewis

The real work of a dream is found in learning how to dream again after life has wrestled the dream away from you by telling you it's not important, it will never happen, you don't have what it takes or you are too old. Excuses thrive in fear and become the paralysis to progress. God didn't have any excuses when it came to giving you the dream so neither should you. God's reason for using you has very little to do with people's opinion and approval of you and more to do with His design in you for people.

Due to age you might be at a stage in life, in which, you may think you are too old to accomplish anything new and that dreaming is a young man's thing. But this just might be the perfect time in your life to now finally live out that dream because you have already accomplished so many other goals. Rather than ruminating on your age, choose to focus on all the years of experience that you now bring to the table that is a result of adolescent trial and error. Your stage is an advantage, not disadvantage.

Let's give a few recent historical examples to give some context that hopefully will help to dispel the notion that the pursuit of a dream has an age limit.

- Asa Candler was a pharmacist that purchased a carbonated drink recipe and 4 years later started the Coca-Cola Company at the age of **41.**

- Sam Walton started Wal-Mart at the age of **44** and later on added Sam's Club.

- Gordon Bowker was a writer who had a dream of roasting coffee beans. Along with two other partners, and at the age of **51**, they started Starbucks and it is now a global icon.

- Harland Sanders (better known as Colonel Sanders) started Kentucky Fried Chicken at the age of **62**!

I recently came across a story that encapsulates the body and spirit of never letting a dream expire. Alan R. Tripp lives in a retirement community in Pennsylvania, and he wrote a poem entitled, "Best Old Friends" at the age of 99 to celebrate the new friends that he was making. When Alan celebrated his 100th birthday, a friend of his at that same retirement community, by the name of Marvin Weisbord, wanted to surprise Alan by putting his poem to music. Little did Alan know but Marvin was an accomplished jazz pianist. Hearing his poem to music inspired Alan to write more poems and to have Marvin collaborate with him regarding the instrumentation.

This unlikely duo began performing their original songs, along with Marvin's band called the Wynlyn Jazz Ensemble, for their neighbors and friends within retirement communities. The music was well-liked because it was written for seniors by seniors with topics and puns that resonated within their community. Their music became so popular, and their new song collection so extensive, that they decided to fulfill a lifelong dream of recording an album. So Alan, at the age of **102,** and Marvin, at the age of **90,** released their first album called, "Senior Song Book."

The dream doesn't have an age requirement. The only thing that age dictates is how long you get to enjoy living in the phenomenon of the dream being realized. So go and don't waste another moment!

…Don't Quit!

"Don't give up. Don't ever give up."
Jimmy Valvano

Discouragement is a loss of confidence or enthusiasm, and it surfaces as an inability to act due to that loss of confidence. It can be debilitating and can ultimately cause you to want to quit. There is nothing wrong in feeling discouraged, but it can become harmful if it is not processed in a healthy way that allows for growth and forward movement. Discouragement is a natural God-given emotion, and I believe that it can have a positive purpose. With any feeling of failure, whether it is personally, professionally, or relationally, there comes a sentiment of defeat. But that moment can also allow for a time to reflect and the opportunity for a reboot.

There will be moments when your plan will not work, the schematic unravels, the bright idea has no current, the breakthrough hits another wall, and simply put the dream is losing its steam. But all is not lost. Take comfort in the fact that it may be part of your process. All dreams, no matter the size, require modifications in order to achieve and maintain its intended performance.

In my experience, people don't have a problem with dreaming; the problem is in believing that the dream can actually become reality. Can I REALLY live in that type of house and drive that kind of car? Can my body REALLY be healed, made over, or lose weight? Can I REALLY have joy, the fairytale ending, live happily ever after? Can I REALLY recover from this public sin, private sin, addictive sin? Can I REALLY be my own boss, own my own business, and employ others? Can I REALLY be good enough to sign that contract, break into that industry, have my own label or firm? Can I?

Our path in life is specific and is unlike no one else's. The journeys are similar, from where we are to where we want to be, but the paths will be different. But we can find encouragement from the stories of others who have journeyed before us that refused to quit! Sometimes the greatest thing you can do today is not quit. We will know of your story because you choose not to quit. Here are six stories of people who refused to give up and the impact they have made or are making on history.

Abraham Lincoln – Abraham Lincoln was a lawyer who lost a total of eight political races, but his losses left him undeterred. Thankfully his tenacity outweighed the disappointment of defeat, and in 1860 he was elected President of the United States of America. The tumultuous experiences of personal defeats forged him into being a leader that could guide the nation through its turbulent times. He was only in office for four years, but many regard him as having one of the most well-respected and successful presidencies in history.

Oprah Winfrey – From her childhood and through her adult career, Oprah's life has been one of not throwing in the towel. She was fired from her first television job because she was too emotionally invested in the people and their stories. But instead of listening to her critics, she followed her heart. Remarkably, Oprah tuned out her critics and continued to pursue human-interest stories. These stories would become her trademarks on her nationally syndicated talk shows. This unwavering conviction to the pursuit of her dream now has her listed as the world's first Black female billionaire. In her 2013 Harvard commencement speech, she shared this: "There is no such thing as failure. Failure is just life trying to move us in another direction."

Henry Ford – Henry was an engineer that watched his first automobile business go bankrupt in 1899. Rather than quit he stayed the course with his ideas because he fundamentally believed in his dream. So Henry re-organized and in 1901 he started the Henry Ford Company. Finally, in 1903, he gained manufacturing success with the Model A, and then again in 1908 with the Model T. And the rest, as they say, IS history.

Vera Wang - After an investment of the adolescent years of her childhood, Vera realized that her dream of Olympic gold as a figure skater would not be realized. And rather than succumb to the failure of one dream, Vera exchanged it for the pursuit of another. Shortly after college she pursued fashion and began working at Vogue, but after spending spent 17 years there she realized that she needed to start her own clothing line because her career was stalling. The lessons she learned from her failures fueled her success as one of the biggest names in wedding dress design and couture. Vera states, "No matter how bad things get, no matter how discouraged I feel, no matter how much of a failure I feel like ... I try to believe there's a reason, there's a process, and there's a learning experience."

Walt Disney – Walt Disney's story is littered with examples of perseverance at every stage. When Walt was in his early 20s, the Kansas City Star fired him because he "lacked imagination and had no good ideas." Despite this criticism Walt continued with his dream of cartooning and he founded a studio, but unfortunately that went bankrupt. Walt began working as an artist at another job, and it was at that drawing board that a new character was created. Disney created Mickey Mouse in his darkest moment after rejection and failure. It is because of not quitting that the world has a vault of iconic Disney cartoons and movies, Disney theme parks, and memories to share from one generation to another. It is romantically said that, "It all started with a mouse…" but we know it started with a man who had a dream and refused to quit.

James Earl Jones – James's father, Robert Earl Jones, left him and his mother when he was 5 years old for New York and Hollywood where he would later become an accomplished actor. The initial rejection by Robert left James's mother so despondent that James had to be raised by his maternal grandparents. The trauma of these events and his eventual move with his grandparents from Mississippi to Michigan caused James to develop a stutter, and consequently he refused to speak. James remained a functional mute for years until he went to high school. It was in high school that his English teacher discovered that he had a gift for writing poetry. His teacher encouraged him to speak his poetry and to end his self-imposed silence. James discovered that his poetry gave him a voice, and he began to speak. At first the sound of his voice was filled with stuttering because he had been silent for so long. But James refused to quit, and with the support of his English teacher, who he credits with helping and encouraging him, he continued to read poetry, which lead to public speaking, which eventually led to acting. Because of this perseverance, James overcame stuttering and during an impressive professional acting career he has won the coveted EGOT (Emmy, Grammy, Oscar and Tony), which has been accomplished by a total of only 15 people. Strangely enough, James Earl Jones is best known as the VOICE of Darth Vader of the Star Wars saga, Mufasa of the Lion King franchise, and the legendary tagline for CNN. This from a young boy who overcame stuttering due to trauma and refused to quit rehearsing even when others felt like he had no voice. Now he is known because of his voice.

Just look at these six examples. These stories are dripping with irony on how the closing of one door leads you to the door of the room where your dream has been patiently waiting all along. You can't let a setback deter you. Success tastes even sweeter when you know what you had to go through to get it.

Every day I wake up, I tell myself that today I am one day closer to the dream being realized. Truthfully, it may take all that I have today to just hold on. But I'm so glad that the Bible tells us in Ephesians 6:13-14,

"Wherefore take the whole armor of God, that you may be able to stand in the evil day, and **having done all, to stand. Stand therefore…"**

So there will be days when the greatest advancement that I can make is one of being clothed in God's grace and having the fortitude and determination to **just stand!** Therefore I make a conscious decision everyday to not quit. It doesn't mean that discouragement won't come, because it will, but I already know that it will not get the last word of my day. I may not get it right all the time, and I will make mistakes, but I will not abandon His trust in me. I have had business ventures fail, a church plant close, car repossessed, house foreclosed on, wages garnished, judgments decreed, death of close loved ones, friends leave, and credit declined, but I refused to quit. Why? Because assessments can be reversed, credit can be repaired, and bad decisions can be fixed, but the dream cannot be attained if you walk off the field. I refuse to quit. Cry? Maybe. Questions? Probably. Anxious? Sometimes. Lament? Definitely. But quit? NEVER!

Defeating Doubt

"Doubt kills more dreams than failure ever will."
UNKNOWN

We all have to encounter doubt. Doubt is a feeling of uncertainty or lack of conviction. Doubt is death to a dream. The reason we doubt the dream is because it was never ours to begin with. In most cases if we could dream our own dream we would have dreamt something different (easier, more within reach, readily attainable, etc.). The dream we have is God's dream for us, and in all cases it will take God to get it done. That's why doubt is so powerful, because if truth were told we really don't want to do it. Sleep is easier, inactivity is more comfortable, and wishing is simpler than the reality of the struggle with disappointment that will come from pursuing a dream.

Doubt is one of the devil's most used tools against the dream, and it must be violently and defiantly defeated with deliberate focus. Stay focused on the dream. Focus is easy to maintain in spurts, but much harder to sustain over a long period of time. Surround yourself with reminders of what God said and what that dream may look like. If your dream is to be an artist, visit an art museum. If your dream is to be an architect, go visit a skyscraper. If your dream is to be a doctor, enroll in an internship. Whatever your dream is, submerse yourself in environments that are the reality of your dream being possible. If your dream is one that has never been accomplished, then connect yourself with people who have been labeled as trailblazers. Immerse yourself in a milieu of those who did things before they were ever done. Your dream is possible, but it is imperative that you surround yourself with other dreamers.

If you want to kill a BIG dream, tell it to a small mind. Even in environments that are full of dreamers, you will find that there are people who can only dream small. They do not have the ability at that moment to dream beyond a certain limit. Their dreams are contained within limitations, and their inability to go beyond that box is dangerous to dreamers who dream big dreams; who believe that the sky is the limit. Small dreamers will unknowingly try to tether your feet to the ground with them. Be careful with your dream and discerning with whom it is shared.

If you want to kill a BIG dream, tell it to a small mind.

Don't Be Afraid to Fail

*"Stop being afraid of what could go wrong,
and start getting excited about what could go right."*
Tony Robbins

Failure is part of the process of development. It helps to make you aware of what won't work so that you can eliminate it from your list and turn your focus elsewhere. Failure is not your enemy, doubt is. Doubt is the fear to even try. If the seed of doubt gets planted and is allowed to germinate, it will grow to be a tree that you fasten a swing to and use to pacify yourself as the days of purpose pass you by; swinging and having the sensation of movement but in reality never progressing beyond that spot. Get off the swing of doubt and take a swing at your dream!

"Do not be afraid..." is written in the Bible 365 times! How providential it is for that statement to be listed the exact number of days we have in a year. From His word, God is giving us a daily reminder to trust Him and to live everyday being fearless.

Dream Scenarios

"When you run a part of the relay and pass on the baton, there is no sense of unfinished business in your mind. There is just the sense of having done your part to the best of your ability. That is it. The hope is to pass on the baton to somebody who will run faster and run a better marathon."
N. R. Narayana Murthy

God has utilized dreams to get man's attention since the beginning of mankind. Dreams were used to warn (present danger) and inform (future and purpose). There are various accounts of God-given dreams recorded in the Bible. The first recorded mention of a dream in the Bible is when God tells King Abimelech to not touch Sarah because she is not Abraham's sister but his wife. In the dream the King is warned that if he touches her he will die. We are also already aware of the dream that was given to Joseph. Dreams continue in the New Testament as God uses a dream to tell Joseph that his betrothed, Mary, is pregnant and that she has not been dishonest regarding the child's conception. In the dream, the angel of the Lord tells Joseph to follow through with his plans and to take Mary as his wife. Subsequently in the same story, the wise men are warned in a dream to not return to King Herod after they discovered the whereabouts of young Jesus. Later on Pilate has to decide whether or not to execute Jesus and in Matthew 27:19, Pilate's wife tells him, *"Don't have anything to do with that innocent man, for I have suffered a great deal today in a dream because of him."* Dreams have often been a catalyst used by God to get His will accomplished on the earth.

As we see in the life of Jesus, dreams were often used as scenes in his life to help ensure that He got to the climax of the journey. There were multiple people who each had a dream that was part of His grand story. In the same light, God gives dreams to individuals to help us all get to the collective highlight of the journey. Our dream is a piece of the story; a crucial piece nevertheless. I believe that there are times in our life that the dream is so heavy because not only are we living out God's dream for us but possibly the dream before us that was dropped by someone else. All of our dreams are pieces of the big puzzle, and they all must be accounted for in order for the picture to make sense. Consequently I believe that sometimes included in our dream is the fallen unfulfilled dream of a father, mother, sister, brother, etc.

In Genesis 28 we find Jacob on the run. Earlier in his life we find that Jacob tricked his older brother Esau into selling him his birthright for a bowl of soup and then, with the help of his mother, tricks his blind dying father into giving him his blessing that he thought he was giving to Esau. When Esau walks in to find that the blessing had been given to Jacob, he is enraged and wants to kill Jacob. Jacob is now fleeing to his uncle's house for safety from his brother Esau. Jacob is a deceiver, a liar, and a trickster, but he is also the grandson of Abraham and now God's plan and purposes are at stake. While on the run, Jacob stops in the desert for a night in order to get some rest. Jacob goes to sleep, and while he is asleep God visits Jacob in a dream.

> *[Jacob] had a dream in which he saw a stairway resting on the earth, with its top reaching to heaven, and the angels of God were ascending and descending on it. There above it stood the Lord, and he said: "I am the Lord, the God of your father Abraham and the God of Isaac. I will give you and your descendants the land on which you are lying. Your descendants will be like the dust of the earth, and you will spread out to the west and to the east, to the north and to the south. All peoples on earth will be blessed through you and your offspring. I am with you and will watch over you wherever you go, and I will bring you back to this land. I will not leave you until I have done what I have promised you."*

Genesis 28:12-15

God uses a dream to reinforce to Jacob that he is part of a bigger picture that began with a promise to his grandfather. In spite of his foolishness and recklessness, God was still going to bless his descendants because of what He promised to his grandfather Abraham and father Isaac. Even though through his own actions he was now on the run from his brother, the end of his story would be one of blessing, protection, and promises fulfilled. In pursuit of dreams and aspirations, we need to be reminded that God has a plan and that we don't need to trick or lie our way into contention. What God has for us is for us!

God's dream to Jacob was to correct his action, be reminded of the blessing and promise to his lineage, and to stay the course. Who would have known that the beginning to the fulfillment of the promise would come through his son, Joseph? That's right, Joseph is the son of Jacob and the great-grandson of Abraham! Joseph had a dream that was specific to him, but it was also part of the broader landscape of God's plan for

God's dream is never about you only; it will always be a part of a larger dream scenario.

humanity. Sometimes, particular details of your dream can be the result of an unfulfilled dream given to another or your stage of the fulfillment of a dream that began before you. God's dream is never about you only; it will always be a part of a larger dream scenario.

Our dream scenario is to carry the fulfilled dream (baton) to the next dreamer (runner) so that we may all finish the race. It may seem unfair that our leg of the race is a little heavier or more burdensome than someone else's, but I must profess that you can handle it. I know what it feels like to carry the weight of what someone else dropped and the hope of those whose piece of the dream scenario is connected to mine. But I have found comfort in knowing that God built me for this and when it becomes too much, I can simply trust that He will pick me up and carry me through what I can't traverse. In Hebrews 12:1-2, the Apostle Paul eloquently explored this idea with a presumptuous metaphor that says,

"Wherefore seeing that we also are compassed about with so great a cloud of witnesses, let us lay aside every weight, and the sin which doth so easily beset us, and let us run with patience the race that is set before us, looking to Jesus the author and finisher of your faith..."

We may not be able to control the start, the route or the circumstances of our dream but we can control one thing...that we finish!

Dreams Have Directions

"If you want to be successful, you have to jump, there's no way around it. When you jump, I can assure you that your parachute will not open right away. But if you do not jump, your parachute will never open. If you're safe, you'll never soar!"
STEVE HARVEY

There is so much to say, so much that can and should be said, but at some point you have to turn off the faucet, drink the water in the cup, and wait to be thirsty again before you turn the faucet back on. Consequently I thought I was finished and was ready to turn the page, but one last thought arose that must be added to this chorus even if it is only just for you and not applicable to anyone else. This last thing is a hard truth I unknowingly lived out and learned the principle later. I think the reason for this is because, as stated earlier, if God showed you the topography of the journey of the dream, many of us would object. Surprisingly enough, this truth was uncovered as I was studying a message for Christmas. Luke 2:4-5 says,

"And Joseph went up from Galilee, out of the city of Nazareth, into Judea, unto the city of David, which is called Bethlehem, because he was of the house and lineage of David, to be registered with Mary, his betrothed wife, who was with him."

On the surface this scripture may seem very benign in nature and not even worth mentioning, as it is an outlier to the context of the story. But there was a phrase that I couldn't shake; *"…Joseph went up from Galilee, out of the city of Nazareth…"* Remember I said in the previous paragraphs that Joseph had a dream and the dream told him to take Mary as his bride and to protect her. Therefore the above scripture is a direct result of his dream. So here is what is gnawing at me; the journey of a dream not only takes you "up from" but it may also require you to go "out of". Let that soak in…

A dream may require movement "up from" and "out of". We all want the "up from" but seldom do we anticipate it might also require the "out of" (a city, a relationship, a town, a group of friends, etc.).

You rarely give birth in the same place that conception took place. Mary conceived Jesus Christ in Galilee, but He was birthed in Bethlehem. God's dream for Mary, and mankind, was conceptualized in one geographical place, but the birth of the dream took place in another region. Just because God gives you a dream in one city doesn't necessarily mean it will be birthed in the same place. Sometimes the dream requires us to move to new places

You rarely give birth in the same place that conception took place.

and new territories. God famously told Abram (Abraham) in Genesis 12:1,

"Get out of your country, from your family, and from your father's house, to a land that I will show you."

In other words, he was not in the place where the dream would come to pass. What God wanted to do for and in Abram (Abraham) couldn't happen where he was, so God needed him to move. Abram (Abraham) had to move, Joseph had to move, Joseph and Mary had to move, and you *may* have to move.

God will never force you to move. He will always give you a choice in the matter. I want you to consider for a moment that it may be possible that the reason your dream hasn't materialized is because you are requiring God to do it where you are while God is requiring you to move to where He is. God blesses you in the place where He has decided for the dream to materialize. Come to grips and be ok with the fact that your stubbornness that was needed to get you to where you are may be the very thing now that is preventing growth. Maybe the store should be in another county, the church on a different block, the business in a different city, the programming for a different group, meeting in some new spaces, finding friends in contrasting circles, or new strategies pursued instead of previous charted courses. All dreams, no matter the size, will require modifications in order to achieve and maintain great performance. The thing that most people resist is change because they are afraid of it. Change requires trust, and we must trust in God to see His dream come to pass in our lives; even if it requires a move.

My journey, up to this point, required that type of move. Thankfully I didn't have to leave my country, but I physically had to leave my father's house and extended family to follow God to an unfamiliar place. If I can be totally honest, the move was traumatic. We lost a lot on the way, but we have discovered so much more. I lost stuff but gained substance. I lost acquaintances but gained friends. I lost things but gained treasure. I lost a form of godliness and gained

God. I lost public prayer invites but gained a private prayer life. I lost stages with people but gained an audience with the King. Where I am now could not have been gained by staying in place.

Replanting is the process of moving a plant from one location to another. Replanting (or transplanting) is used for three primary reasons: extending the growing season, avoiding germination issues, and protection. The protection reason is particularly interesting because it speaks to the protection of young plants until they are sufficiently established. The farmer protects a plant in one environment until its root system is strong enough to handle the elements on its own. God didn't choose to transplant you because you did something wrong. Quite the contrary, you are being transplanted because you are strong enough to handle the move. I can only imagine that for a plant, the process of being plucked up and replanted might be painful, but it produces gains that could never be experienced any other way.

Dreams have the power to move you in ways you never thought were possible. Not only can a dream move you emotionally, euphorically, and mentally, but it can also move you physically. Be careful to not misinterpret the dream for the location you are in. The dream is for a certain space, time and geographical location. In Esther 4:14, Mordecai exhorts his niece (who he raised as his daughter), the queen,

"Yet who knows whether you have come to the kingdom for such a time as this?"

He was imploring her to remember! Remember that the fulfillment of an individual dream will take you to a place for the sake of a collective people. Considering that the dream is bigger than you and for more people than just you can sometimes

Dreams are destinations, and we never know how they'll be routed.

help give you the courage to try and do things that would never have been considered by you if the dream were just for you. A mother re-enrolls in school because she wants a better life not just for her but also for her children and her children's children. A struggling actor will move from the Midwest to California in order to pursue acting opportunities. An attorney will leave the comfort of partnership in order to establish her own firm. A cook leaves an established restaurant in order to be a chef and open his own food truck. Dreams are worth you pursuing wherever they may take you. The journey may be bumpy, but the destination will make it all worthwhile. Dreams are destinations, and we never know how they'll be routed.

Living the Dream

"The real question over our lives is not how strong we will begin our race to pursue God's call but how strong we will finish it. There are far few finishers out there than beginners. Finishers are impressive."
BANNING LIEBSCHER

Pursuing a dream is never easy, but it is necessary. There are selfish reasons for the pursuit: to be an example to others, our conduct would be an encouragement to our children's dreams, for someone to be proud of the accomplishment, personal and public acclaim. But I believe for the majority of people it is because we want to answer the question of, What if? What if I did succeed?! What would my life look like? Whatever your motivation, it is time to roll yourself off of the proverbial couch and dust off that dream. That may be easier said than done, but you must begin somewhere.

The dream must be renewed! As we get older life gets in the way of dreaming. We are told to get our heads out of the clouds, snap back to reality, and get back to the mundane. But we should have been encouraged to dream, and if it failed to then dream bigger next time. Somewhere along the way we began to believe the lie that in order to have a dream tomorrow that we are somehow neglecting today. And tragically we place our dreams on the back burner, with the promise to return to them, but one day turns into a month and a month into a year and a year into a decade, and by the time we look up from our daily routine we find

...we should have been encouraged to dream, and if it failed to then dream bigger next time.

ourselves in a rut that we think is inescapable. Time doesn't still our dream all at once because we would see that coming and defend our dream from it. But systematically a tiny piece is stolen one day at a time: initially unnoticeable but eventually undeniable.

Inexplicably and unintentionally we have traded the dream. We traded extra-ordinary for ordinary, the thrill of new for the consistency of comfortable, stepping out for staying in, and moving forward to retreating silently. We have exchanged our dreams for duties, but today is the day that it must come to an end! Renew the dream by asking God to revisit you with His dream for your life. And know that it is okay to maintain your duties while you also give time to your dream. Pull out those old journals and begin taking new notes. Revisit those old schematics and plans. Re-enroll in school and finish that degree! Stretch those muscles and get back to competition. Believe in yourself again because God never stopped believing in you.

"Being confident of this very thing, that He which began a good work in you will perform it until the day of Jesus Christ:"
Philippians 1:6

There are times when I am on my computer or phone and the screen becomes stuck. It is one of the most frustrating things in the world to me, especially if I am in the middle of trying to complete a task. I sometimes want to fall to my knees and with great passion, resembling a scene from one of my favorite movies, throw my hands up in the air with my fists balled tight and rain coming down all around me and scream, "Why!" After the emotion of the moment passes, I always realize that there is a much simpler solution that has been embedded into my device that helps with such scenarios because the manufacturers knew that this would happen. In the upper corner of every device there is a button that must be engaged. This action refreshes the screen. It simply unsticks what was stuck.

God is the manufacturer of the dream and of us, and He knew that there would be times that we would get stuck. God knows the weight (and wait) of the dream. The weight of the dream is to remind us that we cannot do it without Him and if we could it wouldn't be worth doing. But don't worry, just as there is a refresh button on our device, there is also a refresh button for our lives as well. That refreshing comes from spending time with Him: a time of unveiling our discouragement and frustrations to God; a time of being transparent enough to let God know that we are tired and don't know how much more we can take. It is always in those times of honesty with God that He refreshes us. We come away from that time of prayer and worship revitalized and ready to take on the dream again. Whatever you have to do, make your way into God's presence and let Him restore the joy and passion of the dream.

Day Dreams

"Never give up on a dream just because of the time it will take to accomplish it. The time will pass anyway."
EARL NIGHTINGALE

Daydreaming has been defined as "a dreamlike musing or fantasy while awake, especially of the fulfillment of wishes or hopes...." Some like to say that daydreaming is the musing of lazy people who are trying to escape the reality of their current dire situation. But I see daydreaming not as escapism, but as a creative discovery. Daydreaming can be an incubator for dreamers.

Between the time of the gift of the dream and the realization of the dream is a time I like to call the "meantime." It is the distance between hope and reality, infancy and maturation, nonfulfillment and actualization. And it can really be a "mean" time. The time is mean because the gulf of the gap could be days, weeks, months, or even years. What do you do with that time? If it is not navigated carefully, it can cause you to want to forfeit the whole dream. I believe the secret lies not only in revisiting the dream at night but reviewing the details of the dream during the day. The influence of daydreaming is seen in the adjustments to behaviors and habits that take place during the day to help you achieve what you have been dreaming about at night.

I remember early on in life I had three simple goals that I wanted to achieve and in this order: be married, be a father, and pastor a church. Consequently enough by my mid-twenties I had accomplished all of those goals with varying degrees of success. I quickly realized that I had to create some new goals: brand-new house and brand-new Mercedes Benz! These new goals were dreams because they were things that seemed a lot less attainable due to their price tags. Nevertheless I began to daydream about the house. While living in the apartment with my wife and two children, I daydreamed about the house. While sleeping on bunk beds of family members homes because we lost our apartment, I daydreamed about the house. After getting steady financial footing and acquiring a townhouse rental, I daydreamed about the house. I daydreamed about our house when we went to open houses. I daydreamed about our house when we decided to stop going to open houses of used houses and exclusively started going to new construction. I daydreamed about the house when the bank denied us for a loan. But it was too late because now the house was in me. I already knew where my office was, how big the kitchen was, how many rooms there were, and the color of the paint on the wall. I walked **I walked through it in my daydreams before I ever stepped foot in it.** through it in my daydreams before I ever stepped foot in it. So much so that when the home became a reality it may have been a surprise for others but it had been a reality to me for years.

See, this is the power of daydreaming! Daydreaming about the dream will give you the power of imagination that helps to fill the gulf of time. It is easier to deal with a reality that is opposite of your dream when your vision for the future is sustaining you in the moment. Dream with your eyes wide open and envision the possibilities of what it is going to be like. Imagine what the restaurant is going to look like: the music being played, the smell of the food, the sound of dishes clanging as they are being cleared away from the table to make room for your waiting customers. Imagine the adoption being finalized: the tears on everyone's faces, the joy in your child's face, and the sound of the gavel as it smashes the definitive conclusion to your case. Imagine re-enrolling into school: the rush of signing up for new classes, the exchange of new ideas, the smell of your graduation robe as you put it on in preparation to walk across that stage and get your degree! If you can imagine it, you can realize it!

I am reminded of a time recently when a good friend of mine, Pastor David Wright, reached out to me because God had placed me on his mind. I was so glad he called because I was in a tough place and in need of connection. I was primarily irritated by something that I thought should have happened sooner and in my estimation was unnecessarily taking too long. He patiently listened, and then calmly asked if he could pray. His prayer was filled with wisdom, and I did something that I have never done before while someone prayed for me…I took notes on what was being prayed out. He said that, "God's timing is always perfect…" and then he said something that so resonated with me because it was so practical and innovative at the same time. Pastor David said, "God is working primarily in us, not just through us." What?! That statement, in prayer, made me realize that the journey of the dream (or anything else for that matter) is also about God working something IN us. We are so consumed with God using us and working through us that we forget that He is foremost

> **God is working primarily in us, not just through us.**

concerned with working His word and will IN us first! God's dream for us has to get worked in us first. The delay, journey, trials, failures, emotional roller coasters, etc. is all about God working something in us and other things out of us. I think this thought is captured perfectly in the Bible in James 1:4, *"Let patience have its perfect work, that you may be perfect and complete, lacking nothing."*

There is an infamous statement that says, "Don't quit your day job." Many people have heard this from others throughout their life as they have expressed to a co-worker, friend, family member, or colleague the dream that they have: the dream to leave their current responsibility and to pursue something that is different. Often it is difficult for the person to give support to the idea of the dream because of where they are. Their own dreams may have been discouraged or shattered and out of this disorder they sometimes unknowingly bring discouragement to your doorstep with the aforementioned sarcastic statement. Society tries to diminish your ability to dream so that you can fulfill roles within their dream. But be determined to continue to daydream and dream at night until the dream becomes your reality. Whatever you do, "Don't quit your daydreaming."

Sweet Dreams

"The future belongs to those who believe in the beauty of their dreams."
ELEANOR ROOSEVELT

There is a ritual, which was started by my wife, that takes place every night in our home. Before our children can go to bed, they have to put on their pajamas, brush their teeth, and then say goodnight to us. Each of their nightly gestures is different. Some include secret and special handshakes, hugs, kisses, prayers, etc. All of this is leading to the moment, when on most occasions, my wife walks into their rooms, tucks them into bed, gently kisses them on the head, and we quietly whisper to them, "Sweet dreams." Instantly a smile hits their face as their eyes close and they peacefully wander into sleep. There is security in this practice because they know that our presence signifies security and our affection is their approval. This development marks the end of their day and permission to dream about tomorrow.

In a similar way, God provides the same security and presence for us. We can lay our head down tonight and have sweet dreams, knowing that today may not have been the day we hoped for but tomorrow very well may be. We can rest our head on the pillow of quietness and wrap ourselves in the blanket of contentment knowing that according to Zephaniah 3:17, *"...He will quiet (me) with His love, He will rejoice over (me) with singing."*

Furthermore you can rest knowing that, according to Psalm 121:4, *"He who keeps Israel shall neither slumber nor sleep."*

My hope and prayer for you, and for all of us, is that this book has provided the gentle (or not so gentle) nudge (or push) to get us to have the courage to revisit the dream that God gave to us. My prayer is that when you close your eyes tonight that your sleep is filled with visions of your dream being accomplished and your day is overflowing with creative innovations as you walk it out before you step into it. May you be surrounded by like-minded people who know how to celebrate, collaborate, encourage, and cheer for you! May you also be able to navigate the terrain of detractors who are grappling with their own shortcomings and still learning how to value the dreams of others. May you continue to dream during the day and night, and may those dreams be sweet dreams. May you continue to fight for the dream until you hold the dream in your hands. May you never underestimate the life-changing and paradigm-shifting power of your dream. May you always know that your dream was first God's dream for you!

And just as Joseph's story was for me, may this book be an inspiration for you to Dream Again.

The End.

~~The End.~~

The Beginning…

Dream Again!

Chapter 6 Reflections

"You are never too old to set another goal or to dream a new dream."
C.S. Lewis

Meditate on these scripture verses:

James 1:2-4, 1 Corinthians 1:27, Ephesians 6:13-14, Genesis 28:12-15, Luke 2:4-5

Reflect:

- Your dream is a collective of every experience.

- It's not too late!

- If you want to kill a BIG dream, tell it to a small mind.

- You rarely give birth in the same place that conception took place.

- "I walked through it in my daydreams before I ever stepped foot in it." – Jason N. Turner

Questions:

What is your favorite excuse? How often have you told yourself, and others, that excuse? What do you daydream about? Where did you place your timeworn dream and are you still able to retrieve it so that you can renew it in this season? How does the prospect of a renewed dream move you?

_____

_____

_____

_____

_____

Prayer:

"Father help me to dream again. Help me to push past the failures and hurt. Help me to see you in every step of this journey. Help me to not lean to my own understanding but in all my ways to acknowledge you because I know you will direct my path. Help me to push past discouragement and regret. Help me to not harbor ill feelings in my heart of those who promised things and didn't deliver. Help me to see that you were in it all, gently pushing me closer to your arms. Your love for me is inescapable and I am glad that it is more than enough. Thank you for believing in me when I couldn't. Thank you for seeing the best in me and entrusting me with this dream. I will dream again! In Jesus name. Amen."

Activity:

Make a list of your current accomplishments. Now think back to the failures that precipitated them and write them next to the accomplishment. In review you will see that a setback always came before the victory and every time you persuaded yourself to push ahead. This dream is no different, only that it is bigger. Consequently, it will require not only your push but the push of your community, friends, and God.

Now write a list of the small group of friends you can count on to push you through with encouragement and prayer to the finish line of your dream!

_____

_____

_____

_____

_____

_____

_____

_____

7

EPILOGUE

The Phone Rings

I answered the phone, and I heard my mother's voice, but I could tell that something was wrong. It was my grandmother, and she was in hospice care and things were starting to deteriorate. The day we knew was coming was here, and my grandmother would shortly be leaving this earth to spend an eternity for the one in whom she believed in and lived for. We all flew to the Midwest to attend the funeral and to be with our family and to celebrate our matriarch.

After the service we loaded up in the truck and took the hour drive back to the hotel. I had been asked to stay over and preach Sunday morning at another church, but after the emotional roller coaster it was having to deliver the eulogy for my grandmother, I surmised that I emotionally didn't have enough of what would be needed to minister to another congregation. Plus, I really felt led to be with my branch of the family tree: my mom, my wife, my children, my sister, and nephew.

The next morning, we collectively headed to church before flying back home to the Southwest. Church was great! We worshipped together, laughed and cried together. We connected with dear friends and had a glorious morning. After church we went to brunch, where my mother was dissatisfied with her meal, and we had a great time as a family. For the most part there were few places where my mom wasn't dissatisfied with her meal. Because she was always critiquing on how the dish could have been prepared better and she would let us know.

We hugged and kissed each other and commented on how we would see each other in church next Sunday at home in Arizona. But next Sunday never came. Who would have known that this was going to be our last time together.

The Phone Rings Again

Sunday afternoon the phone rings. I didn't want to answer the phone because I could tell something was wrong. This may sound crazy, but the ring was different. This time when I answer the phone it's my sister and something is wrong with mom. Twelve days later the unimaginable has happened and MY mom dies. This can't be happening! My sister and I lose our grandmother and mother within a 30-day period!!

Hats, Furs, and Books

After my mom's virtual funeral, my wife and sister had the arduous task of going through and sorting some of my mom's most valued possessions—her hats and furs. My mom loved to get all gussied-up for church. It was challenging for her to do it in Phoenix because it is considerably hotter here than it was in Wisconsin and Illinois. But she always managed to find a way to punch some flair into her environment, and every now and again we would look up Sunday morning to find my mom walking into church with one of her prized hats. Maybe she couldn't wear the furs, but she was going to wearing her hats.

Consequently, I was given the task to go through her books. It is said you can tell what is on someone's mind by looking at their library. And I must say that going through my mom's library of books I discovered something was on her mind that I never knew. My mother had a dream of being a chef, owning a catering business or restaurant, and writing a cookbook. It was going through her dream that I realized that I had to finish this book, I had to Dream Again. I didn't realize that the deaths of my grandmother and mother had so taken the wind out of me that I hadn't picked up the manuscript of this book in over two months. How could I muster the writing acumen to communicate another line about dreams when one of my dreams had seemingly been crushed. You see, I had always dreamt of purchasing a house with a casita so that my mom could move in with us but still have her own space. I wanted to help relieve the pressure of monthly financial responsibilities so that my mom could live life without the concern over how she was going to manage to pay bills. I wanted her to just enjoy the sun, drive around in her red Cadillac, and cook whatever she wanted, whenever she wanted. Her death robbed me of that dream. And now I find myself having to Dream Again, without my mother.

My mom fulfilled a lot of her dreams. Her work allowed her to travel to 47 of the 50 United States. She had two children that she was extremely proud of. She became a grandmother to five beautiful grandchildren. She graduated from college with a bachelor's degree in Theology. Recently she moved to Arizona, most importantly to be around her children and grandchildren, but also to live out her days in the sun. And she was finally able to get her dream car, a red Cadillac. Even though I had dreams for her and with her, she had her own dreams. And quiet as it was kept, she was working on her latest dream, a cookbook. Even though that dream didn't make it to the finish line, her life is an example of all the other dreams that were accomplished, in spite of the hardships.

Unfinished Business

"You can't go back and change the beginning, but you can start where you are and change the ending."
C.S. Lewis

With tears in my eyes I know I have to make a decision regarding my own dreams. Do I allow the devastating losses that I have experienced deter me from completing a dream that has been years in the making, or do I allow the memory of the force of nature these two beautiful women were to my life to drive me forward and to finish what I started? I realized that just because one dream didn't materialize that it didn't mean it was ok to let other dreams become dormant. So I decided to finish the unfinished business. This time I picked up the manuscript of *Dream Again*, not to critique or edit it, but to be healed by it. Because this time I was in need of the encouragement to dream again.

A few weeks ago, I am on Facebook and I see a post from a colleague back in the Midwest that caught my attention. Timisha Swan-Stewart's post was asking people, "What did you believe you would become before someone told you that you couldn't or wouldn't do it?" And the responses were heartbreaking. To see and hear of all the shattered or deferred dreams that were a result of life and the negative responses from other people. But Timisha did an incredible thing with the comments. She responded back to everyone, and I mean everyone, and encouraged them to get back at it and to pursue their dream with comments like these: "I believe in you…you can do it…what's stopping you now!"

Who knows whether that forum and discussion encouraged those people to get back at it, but I can tell you it did it for me! I immediately got up, went back to my computer and finished the remainder of this book. You are reading this book now because I read a post from Timisha that encouraged me in a rough space to finish the unfinished business. Furthermore, that post caused me to see that this story is needed because people, including myself, need encouragement to finish the unfinished business.

I am not lazy by any means, but I now know from personal experience that unexpected and tragic things can pop up in your life that will take your breath away. And you need someone to be in that space with you that will give you the time to catch your breath. And then will extend a hand to you to help pull you up out of that defining moment. So, allow me from a place of empathy and prayer, to encourage you to get back at it. I know the pain is deep and the loss can't be calculated, but the sun does rise again, and your dream is not over. Muster all the strength you can and go after it again. You may have to do it through tears, but dream again. You may have to push past people's opinions of you, but dream again. You may have to press past the internal echoes of negative comments, but dream again. You may have to pick yourself up from some failure, but dream again. You may have to do it all by yourself, but dream again. You may have to endure discomfort, but dream again. You may have to forgive the ones who hurt you, but dream again. You may be financially broke and physically broken, but dream again! Your heart may be torn to pieces, but dream again! Go ahead, I dare you to dream again and see what God does with it.

The world is waiting for you…Dream Again.

Chapter 7 Reflections

"You can't go back and change the beginning, but you can start where you are and change the ending."
C.S. LEWIS

Meditate on this scripture verse:

Being confident of this very thing, that He which hath begun a good work in you will perform it until the day of Jesus Christ. Philippians 1:6

Reflect:

- Never take the time you have with your family for granted.
- Tragedy can take the wind out of you but don't let it take the dream from you.
- The world is waiting for you…dream again!

Questions:

What unfinished business do you have regarding your dream? What is your plan to finish strong? Who else is dependent upon you realizing your dream?

_____

_____

_____

_____

_____

_____

_____

_____

_____

_____

_____

_____

_____

_____

_____

_____

Prayer:

"Father help me to know that you have a plan for my life that is a result of your dreams for me. Help me to believe that I am worth that dream and that you did not make a mistake in entrusting this dream to me. Father I admit that life has tried its best to break my desire to dream and at times I have given in to the discouragement. But I commit to you today that as you reignite within me your dreams for me, I will trust you to give me the strength and courage to see them through to the end. Thank you for grace and mercy that are new every day. In Jesus name. Amen."

Activity:

When you begin to see what you are doing as having a generational impact then it changes the urgency and the importance of the assignment of your dream.

Make an outline of your dream on a mirror or wall. The outline should reflect the realization of your dream. So, if your dream is a restaurant, then it could be the outline of a building. Maybe your dream is to be an author then your outline could be of a book.

Next, on an individual sticky note write down one way you see your dream impacting you and the future generations of your family's timeline?

Once completed, place that sticky note within the outline on the wall or mirror. Each time you think of something write it on that sticky note and place it in the outline. Over time that outline will be filled with notes to you on why you need to keep going. It will be a continual reminder to you to dream again!

Begin by writing a few notes below and later transfer them to sticky notes.

_____

_____

_____

_____

_____

_____

_____

_____

_____

_____

_____

_____

_____

_____

_____

_____

_____

_____

NOTES

1. Wikipedia contributors, "George Washington Carver," Wikipedia, The Free Encyclopedia, https://en.wikipedia.org/w/index. php?title=George_Washington_Carver&oldid=976766094.

2. Hannah Natanson, "Senior Song Book," Washington Post, December 2, 2019, https:// www.washingtonpost.com/lifestyle/2019/12/02/ these-two-men-just-released-their-first-music-album-age/

3. Presented by Strayer, If These 10 People Had Given Up, The World Would Be Totally Different, A Plus article, October 5, 2016, https://staging.aplus.com/a/10-people-whose-failure-led-to-success?no_monetization=true.

4. Wikipedia contributors, "James Earl Jones," Wikipedia, The Free Encyclopedia, https://en.wikipedia.org/w/index. php?title=James_Earl_Jones&oldid=977400670.

Dictionary References

1. Oxford English Dictionary Online. June 2020. Oxford University Press. http://www.oed.com/viewdictionaryentry/Entry11125